The Rise and Fall of
Fast Track Trade Authority

Updated and Expanded Edition

Lori Wallach

Public Citizen's Global Trade Watch

ISBN: 978-1-58231-052-7

Public Citizen is a nonprofit membership organization in Washington, D.C., dedicated to advancing the public interest through research, publications, information services, litigation and lobbying. Public Citizen advocates for corporate and government accountability, consumer rights in the marketplace, safe and secure health care, fair trade, and clean and safe energy sources. Visit our web page at http://www.citizen.org.

Acknowledgments: Chapters 1 through 4 of this book were authored by Todd Tucker for the 2008-09 edition, and remain mostly unchanged. Tucker was research director of Public Citizen's Global Trade Watch until 2012. He is author of dozens of reports on the World Trade Organization, the North American Free Trade Agreement, and other trade, investment, consumer and economic issues. A graduate of George Washington University, he received his masters from Cambridge University where he is currently pursuing his Ph.D. Tucker conducted much of the primary research for the book's earlier edition, with assistance from Lauren Forbes. Amy Bruno, Isaac Raisner and Rebecca Riddell provided research assistance. Thanks to Heather Boushey, Sarah Edelman, Bill Holland, Kate Pollard, Adina Rosenbaum and Brandon Wu for additional support. Thanks to Steve Charnovitz, Alfred Eckes, Ben Francis-Fallon, James Galbraith, Allen Matusow and Rick Perlstein for their historical insights. GTW Research Director Ben Beachy provided very thoughtful comments on the revision of the book, as did several peer review readers. A helpful overall edit and copyediting for the revised edition was provided by Dolores Byrnes. The author is solely responsible for the book's content.

Additional copies of this book are available from:
Public Citizen's Global Trade Watch
215 Pennsylvania Ave SE, Washington, DC 20003
(202) 546-4996
Price $15.00

About the Book

Under the U.S. Constitution, Congress writes the laws and sets our trade policy. And so it was for 200 years. Yet, over the last few decades, presidents have increasingly taken over both of those powers through a mechanism known as Fast Track.

Fast Track, first established in 1974, delegates to the executive branch five major elements of congressional authority: the power to select trade partners; the power to set terms and sign agreements before Congress votes on them; the authority to write implementing legislation, skirt congressional committee review and amendment processes and directly submit it for a vote; the power to override congressional leaders' control of House and Senate floor schedules and force votes within a set number of days; and an override of normal voting procedures, including a ban on all amendments and limits on debate.

Despite this dramatic shift in the balance of powers between the branches of government, Fast Track's extraordinary seizure of congressional authority has occurred in the context of an arcane procedural mechanism and thus received little scrutiny – until recently.

Fast Track facilitated controversial commercial pacts including the North American Free Trade Agreement (NAFTA) and the World Trade Organization (WTO). Unlike past trade agreements, which were limited to traditional trade matters such as cutting tariffs and opening quotas, these agreements and those that followed NAFTA and WTO set binding restrictions on many U.S. non-trade policies. This includes agreements pertaining to procurement and immigration, financial and energy regulation, patent and copyright law and food and product safety.

In recent years, the use of Fast Track by Democratic and Republican administrations alike to "diplomatically legislate" significant changes to U.S. domestic non-trade laws, and internationally preempt state policies has made the process increasingly controversial.

This updated and expanded edition of "Rise and Fall" explores how the process of designing U.S. trade agreements has changed from

1789 to the present. This book provides unprecedented documentation of the arguments that motivated both opponents and proponents of the expansion of executive power. The last congressional delegation of Fast Track authority terminated in 2007. As some policymakers in Washington consider renewing this flawed procedure, the book considers a new delegation mechanism that could restore a more robust role for Congress and reduce political tension about trade policy.

At issue is what trade agreement negotiating and approval process can best secure prosperity for the greatest number of Americans, while preserving the vital tenets of American democracy and our constitutional checks and balances in the era of globalization.

About the Author

Lori Wallach is the director and founder of Public Citizen's Global Trade Watch (GTW) and coauthor of "Whose Trade Organization? A Comprehensive Guide to the WTO" (The New Press, 2004). A widely cited trade and globalization policy expert, Wallach has testified before Congress, federal agencies, and foreign legislatures. She graduated from Wellesley College and Harvard Law School.

Praise for the 2009 edition of "Rise and Fall"

Senator Sherrod Brown, Democrat of Ohio and congressional trade-policy leader:

> "If you wonder why trade policy over the past several years has reflected such narrow interests, look no further than the imbalanced trade policymaking process that is Fast Track. There is no other legislative mechanism with such extraordinary powers. Read this informed and engaging account of Fast Track's history and take action."

Representative Mike Michaud, Democrat of Maine and Chair of the House Trade Working Group:

> "Most people now in Congress weren't elected when President Nixon designed Fast Track to grab Congress' exclusive constitutional authority over U.S. trade policy. President Obama discussed the need to replace Fast Track with a process that ensures a greater role for Congress. This book provides the lessons of 233 years of American trade authority history to inform Congress's efforts to create just such a new trade negotiating mechanism."

Dean Baker, Co-Director of the Center for Economic and Policy Research, author of "Plunder and Blunder: The Rise and Fall of the Bubble Economy." :

> "This is a valuable account of the process through which business interests have sought to preempt the democratic control of trade policy. These interests have succeeded in structuring the trade debate so that their policies, many of which are highly protectionist, are dubbed 'free trade,' and any opposition is defined as 'protectionist.'"

David Sirota, Syndicated columnist and author of "The Uprising" and "Hostile Takeover.":

> "Trade is one of the most misunderstood yet most important economic issues America confronts in the 21st century – and rescuing our trade policy from the jaws of corporate manipulation must be a top priority for our nation. Lori Wallach and Todd Tucker have provided a much-needed blueprint detailing how we can do just that."

Ha-Joon Chang, University of Cambridge Economics Professor, and author of "Bad Samaritans.":

> "Unbeknownst to most of us, the Fast Track trade authority has been one of the most important institutions that have shaped the global economy in the last few decades. This short but powerful book provides a very detailed, historically informed, and trenchant analysis of this important but neglected issue. It is a must read for anyone who is interested in understanding the future of the U.S. economy and the world economy."

Alfred E. Eckes, Ohio Eminent Research Professor in Contemporary History at Ohio University, author of "Opening America's Market: U.S. Foreign Trade Policy Since 1776," and former Reagan-appointed Chairman and Commissioner, U.S. International Trade Commission:

> "Candidates for federal office should be required to read and address the critical issues raised in this stimulating book. Wallach and Tucker make a persuasive case that the fast-track trade negotiating process produces agreements weighted to the interests of corporate giants and harmful to democratic governance and public safety. Their argument that a more democratic trade policy process is both possible and desirable merits the attention of public officials and thoughtful citizens everywhere."

Peter Riggs, Director of Forum on Democracy & Trade:

> "'The Rise and Fall of Fast Track' takes as its starting point the Constitutional division of authority over commerce and foreign relations between Congress and the President. The authors show how this in-built tension – Congress safeguarding its right to regulate Commerce, the President arguing for deference to his broader foreign policy objectives – has played out in different political contexts and climates. The result is a fascinating narrative of committee influences and political personalities, of short-term electoral advantage and how the United States' evolving role in the global economy increased the ambition of the executive branch. Most importantly, 'The

Rise and Fall' shows the highly contingent nature of the current Nixon-era template for delegating power to the President, its eventual exhaustion under George W. Bush, and its failure to provide a suitable basis for trade policy formation in the future. Tucker and Wallach's highly readable account gives us the historical grounding necessary for re-thinking Congress' role in negotiating and implementing trade agreements, one that restores a healthy balance of powers, more consistent with our system of Constitutional federalism."

The Rise and Fall of Fast Track Trade Authority

Table of Contents

Introduction

The U.S. Constitution creates "checks and balances" designed to ensure that no single branch of government has undue power over the others. Regarding trade policy, the legislative branch – Congress – has exclusive authority "to regulate commerce with foreign nations" and to "lay and collect taxes [and] duties."[1] The executive branch – the president and his administration – has exclusive authority to negotiate international agreements with foreign sovereigns. In other words, under the Constitution, the president may negotiate international trade agreements at will, but the United States can only be bound to a trade agreement through a vote of Congress.

Throughout the years, Congress has created various means to coordinate the trade-agreement roles of the legislative and executive branches. Congress has the authority to determine how the executive branch will cooperate with Congress on trade agreement negotiations because Congress has exclusive constitutional authority over setting the policy in this area. This is a point worth noting. Many now in Congress have no experience of how trade agreements were created prior to 1975, when the first grant of Fast Track went into effect and dramatically shifted control of the process to the executive branch.

During most of the nation's history, Congress maintained tight control over the content of trade agreements. Congress instructed executive branch officials to negotiate specific tariff cuts or other trade terms for specific products with specific countries and then adopted changes to U.S. tariff rates or other trade policies through a vote of Congress. Starting with the 1934 Reciprocal Trade Agreements Act, Congress has agreed to a variety of mechanisms to delegate to the president what became ever-expanding aspects of its constitutional trade authority, initially by authorizing the president to *proclaim* tariff modifications within certain congressionally-set limits.

---

1. U.S. Constitution, Article I Section 8.

1

In some cases – most recently from 1967-75, 1995-2002 and 2007-present – Congress made no delegation of its authority whatsoever. Yet U.S. trade has expanded and trade agreements have proliferated under each of five distinct regimes of congressional-executive coordination on trade negotiations, as well as during periods when no coordination mechanism was in place.

The trade delegation mechanism known by most people today, and the focus of much of this book, is Fast Track, which was established in the 1973-75 period. Fast Track strictly limited Congress' role in the formative aspects of trade agreements. However, perhaps the most critical difference between this and all previous delegation regimes was that *Fast Track also authorized executive-branch officials also to set U.S. policy on non-tariff, and indeed non-trade, issues in the context of "trade" negotiations.* This feature of Fast Track meant that the executive branch obtained expansive authority to set policies on many non-trade issues that would otherwise be under the control of Congress and state legislatures.

Relative to other past U.S. trade-agreement negotiating and approval processes, Fast Track resulted in an extraordinary shift in the relative power between the branches. Under Fast Track, Congress authorized the president unilaterally to choose partners for international agreements that go beyond traditional trade matters, determine the contents of such agreements, and sign the United States up to the terms of the deal... all *before* Congress had a vote. In delegating Fast Track authority, Congress set negotiating objectives, but these were not mandatory and were regularly ignored by executive branch officials. The executive branch was required to give Congress notice of its intent to initiate negotiations and to enter into an agreement. And, the executive branch was required to consult with various congressional committees during negotiations. However, Congress retained no authority to override the executive branch's decisions regarding with which countries negotiations should be initiated nor to stop the executive branch from signing agreements that did not meet congressional objectives. Thus, Congress was effectively removed from the formative aspects of trade agreement development. Under Fast Track, two hundred years of congressional control over U.S. trade policy was reversed: the executive branch was able to unilaterally decide on trade agreement partners and agreement contents and then deliver completed, signed trade agreements to Congress. Only then did Congress have a role.

Yet, under Fast Track, that end-game role was also strictly limited. The mechanism preset special rules for congressional consideration of such pacts, allowing the executive to write implementing legislation, while circumventing normal congressional-committee processes. Specifically, the president could submit an executive-branch-written bill that approved the agreement's contents and all changes to U.S. law needed to conform the agreement's terms for a mandatory vote within a set number of days. Fast Track also preset congressional floor consideration rules for such bills: all amendments were forbidden, normal Senate rules waived, and debate was limited in both chambers of Congress.

Moreover, once these executive-initiated agreements are approved by Congress, existing domestic laws, regulations and administrative procedures must be brought into conformity with the agreement's terms and future such policies must also meet the agreements' terms, even in cases of policy that have nothing to do with trade. For instance, the operative provision of the Agreement Establishing the World Trade Organization requires: "Each Member shall ensure the conformity of its laws, regulations and administrative procedures with its obligations as provided in the annexed Agreements."[2] Failure to conform domestic policies can result in trade sanctions that remain in place until policies are brought into compliance with trade pact terms. And, changes to the agreements' terms can only be made by consensus of all signatory countries. Thus, today's wide-ranging "trade" agreements represent a form of enforceable international governance that is not easily susceptible to modification as U.S. presidents, Congresses or public opinion change.

---

2. Agreement Establishing the World Trade Organization Article XVI-4.

3

Proponents of Fast Track argued that such an extraordinary delegation of congressional authority was needed for executive branch officials to negotiate trade agreements successfully. First, they noted that members of Congress would focus on protecting local industries and interests and thus undermine executive branch officials' ability to make the trade-offs needed to complete wide-ranging deals. Second, they argued that other countries would not dedicate the considerable resources required to negotiate a U.S. trade agreement if Congress could later amend it. Effectively, they argued that for the trade agreement context, a mechanism was needed to transform the U.S. model of government based on checks and balances between separate branches of government into a system closer to the parliamentary system in which the signing of an agreement was tantamount to the approval of an agreement. Third, they noted that as the scope of subjects covered in "trade" negotiations expanded exponentially, the process had become too complex for Congress to micromanage. Essentially, they pointed out that it would not be possible for executive branch officials to negotiate simultaneously both with other countries and with Congress.

Since Congress first approved Fast Track in 1974 (it was signed into law the following year), Congress has delegated Fast Track authority on five additional occasions. It has been employed 16 times among the hundreds of U.S. trade and commercial agreements completed since the mid 1970s. Contrary to the claims made by Fast Track proponents, numerous countries have in fact allocated resources to negotiating trade agreements with the United States without Fast Track procedures being applied. This includes major multilateral agreements, such as the WTO Telecommunication Agreement and the WTO Financial Services Agreement, as well as literally hundreds of bilateral agreements since the 1990s alone.

Congress' decision to grant China Permanent Most Favored Nation (MFN) status and facilitate its entry into the WTO, an extremely controversial and high-impact trade policy decision, also occurred outside of the Fast Track process. Congress had a greater role in directing the terms for bilateral U.S. negotiations with China on WTO accession terms and the grant of permanent MFN status occurred under normal congressional rules. Indeed, President Clinton only had Fast Track authority for two of his eight years and only used it twice, yet among the accomplishments identified by his administration were enactment of hundreds of trade and commercial agreements with diverse countries. As former Clinton administration U.S. Trade Representative Charlene Barshefsky said in 2000, "if you look at our record on trade since 1995, I don't think the lack of Fast Track impeded our ability to achieve our major trade goals."[3] The enormous appeal for other countries of enhanced access to the massive U.S. market and the prestige associated with having a trade agreement with the United States means that countries lined up seeking to initiate U.S. trade agreement negotiations, regardless of whether Fast Track or any other delegation of Congress' constitutional trade authority was in effect.

A more nuanced version of Fast Track proponents' claims about why the procedure is necessary might be that it is required for certain types of agreements – those that contain expansive non-trade provisions that majorities in Congress would oppose and those that are with countries that Congress would not select as U.S. trade agreement partners. Indeed, Fast Track enabled negotiation, signing and passage of the most controversial pacts, such as the Uruguay Round of the General Agreement on Tariffs and Trade (GATT) that established the World Trade Organization (WTO) and the expansive terms covering non-trade policy matters that are enforced by the WTO, as well as the North American Free Trade Agreement (NAFTA) and the Central America Free Trade Agreement (CAFTA).[4]

In contrast, the U.S.-Jordan Free Trade Agreement (FTA) was negotiated and approved by Congress during a period when Congress had not delegated Fast Track authority to the executive branch. The agreement included enhanced labor standards, did not contain most of the controversial non-trade provisions found in other U.S. FTAs, and did not engender the congressional or public opposition that pacts such as NAFTA, WTO and CAFTA faced. Indeed, this FTA was passed in the U.S. House of Representatives by voice vote under normal rules.

---

3. Quoted in Shapiro, 2006, at 79.
4. Other uses of Fast Track included for the GATT Tokyo Round, and FTAs with Israel, Canada, Chile, Singapore, Australia, Morocco, Bahrain, Oman, Peru, Korea, Panama and Colombia.

Many analysts have presented views about the *economic* impacts of Fast Track-enabled trade pacts, which have also become a subject of heated debate in recent elections as American public opinion shifted solidly against pacts such as NAFTA.[5] However, how Fast Track conflicted with fundamental tenets of American governance remains, to date, far less understood and discussed.

Fast Track dramatically altered the balance of powers between the branches in favor of the executive branch and between the federal government and state governments in favor of the executive branch of the federal government. Consider only one aspect of Fast Track's shift of power towards the executive branch - the authority for the executive branch to write legislation that circumvents congressional committee "mark up" amendment processes and to submit directly to Congress a bill on which Congress is obligated to vote within a set number of days. This alone is a stunning derogation of constitutional norms. Fast Track is the only circumstance under which the executive branch obtains the most legislative of all authorities, those of writing legislation and controlling the terms of congressional floor consideration. This aspect of Fast Track led one trade observer to call the mechanism "a legislative laxative that is bad for the U.S. Constitution." And, once adopted by Congress, the trade agreement terms become federal law, and thus preempt state law.

The federal government is obligated to use all constitutionally available means – litigation, additional preempting legislation and removal of federal government funds – to enforce compliance to the pacts' expansive non-trade terms by states.[6]

---

5. Bivens, 2008; Weisbrot, Baker and Rosnick, 2006; Tucker, 2006b; IFTC, 2007; Public Citizen 2008; Tucker 2008; Tucker 2010.

6. See e.g. GATT, UNITED STATES - MEASURES AFFECTING ALCOHOLIC AND MALT BEVERAGES, *Report of the Panel adopted on 19 June 1992, (DS23/R - 39S/206)* at para. 5.45: "The Panel noted in this respect that both parties agreed that under United States constitutional law GATT law is part of United States federal law and, being based on the Commerce Clause of the Constitution, overrides, as a general matter, inconsistent state law. This was also the view of two eminent writers on the law of the GATT, Professors John Jackson and Robert Hudec, to whom Canada and the United States referred in their submissions. In his 1969 treatise, World Trade and the Law of GATT, Professor Jackson comments: "In those nations where it has been settled that valid federal executive regulation is superior to local law, such as the United States, GATT obligates a contracting party's executive to prevent local laws or actions that would violate GATT... ".[16] [Footnote 16: Jackson, John, World Trade and the Law of GATT (1969), page 116.]

Disturbingly, Fast Track's enormous implications for governance extended considerably further in the post-NAFTA-WTO context. Starting with those agreements, "trade" negotiations began to include binding terms with respect to wide swaths of non-trade policy. The resulting agreements set enforceable international law on numerous non-trade matters that is indefinitely binding on future Congresses and state legislatures.

When the Nixon administration first lobbied Congress for Fast Track authority, it maintained that the executive branch would only pursue trade pact terms on very limited non-tariff issues closely related to trade. Instead, over the last 40 years, the scope and content of "trade" agreements have been quietly but dramatically transformed. These agreements are now wide-ranging international commercial pacts containing hundreds of pages of non-tariff provisions that set policy on many non-trade matters traditionally reserved for Congress and state legislatures. The result is that today's "trade" agreements have systematically shifted decision-making on numerous non-trade policies away from the control of local, state and national legislatures to the executive branch and then on to foreign venues impervious to meaningful participation by those who will live with the results.

Indeed, in practical terms, Fast Track provided a means for the president to "diplomatically legislate" on an array of non-trade matters that are sensitive for Republicans and Democrats alike. The mechanism allowed successive presidents since Nixon to establish via international negotiation rules binding on Congress that relate to domestic patent and copyright policy; immigration and visa policy; service-sector policies from energy and transportation to finance and healthcare; food and products safety standards; creation of limits on local development and land-use policy; establishment of new rights and greater protections for foreign investors operating within the United States that extend beyond U.S. law; and even limits on how U.S. tax dollars may be spent in government procurement.

And, Fast Track allowed presidents to lock in such policies. Trade agreement rules are only alterable by consensus of all governments involved in a particular agreement, meaning they have permanence unlike that of domestic policies which future Congresses and state legislatures can alter or eliminate.

Thus, Fast Track operated as a very elegant modern Trojan-horse device. With the outward (welcome) appearance of delivering trade expansion, Fast Track has been used to insert a legion of policies previously repelled by Congress and state legislatures. The Trojan analogy only goes so far in this instance, however, because Congress was complicit in *constructing* the very horse used to attack the inner sanctum of Congress' constitutional authority over non-trade domestic policy.

Moreover, because of the prominent U.S. international role, the shift in the *domestic* balance of power has had *global* implications. Trade agreements established under the broad Fast Track delegation of Congress' authority have established a system of enforceable global governance. The WTO's first director-general described the WTO as "the constitution of a single global economy."[7]

Given bipartisan congressional concerns about sovereignty and maintaining legislative branch prerogatives, how did this come to pass? Fast Track was sold to Congress as being necessary to conclude trade agreements. And, the agreements were sold to Congress and the public as *trade* agreements that would expand U.S. exports, as if the expansive non-trade terms did not exist. With Fast Track relegating Congress to a post-signing vote on lengthy agreements completed by the executive branch and no formal role for most congressional committees in the formative aspects of the rules, many in Congress were simply unaware. Indeed, even today when the WTO or NAFTA rules against a U.S. non-trade policy and orders it to be changed to comply with trade agreement rules, members of Congress contact Public Citizen to inquire: how is this possible? Of course, Fast Track is not solely responsible for the lack of congressional understanding of the pacts' full implications. It is worth considering that when Congress

---

7. "We are no longer writing the rules of interaction among separate national economies. We are writing the constitution of a single global economy." Statement of WTO Director-General Renato Ruggiero at an August 1996 UNCTAD conference. UNCTAD, 1996.

considered approval of the WTO, only one senator was willing to state that he had read the WTO text and answer simple questions about it.[8]

In this book, we tell the story of how the trade-agreement negotiation and approval process evolved in five acts – each representing a distinct regime of how Congress and the executive coordinated their trade-policy roles. Each "act" had its milestone achievements, followed by moments of crisis that resulted in the establishment of a new coordination system.

The first regime, dating from 1789 to 1890, was the longest lasting, and consisted of exclusive congressional control over trade policy. In this period, America went from being an agricultural outpost to a developed nation on par with Europe. There were practically no trade "agreements" during this period; rather, Congress enacted tariff legislation establishing trade terms with various countries with which Congress had instructed executive branch officials to negotiate. The second regime, dating from 1890 to 1934, was a period of congressional experimentation with forms of delegated trade negotiating authority, primarily to allow the executive to penalize imperial European nations who sought to keep U.S. exports out of developing-nation markets. This period ended in the Great Depression, at a time when heads of state around the world were centralizing power. The third regime, dating from 1934 to 1967, was a period of nearly exclusive executive control over trade agreements. Congress explicitly limited the delegation of its constitutional trade authority to tariff rates, establishing a new authority for executive branch negotiators to sign agreements cutting tariffs within bands of congressionally-set rates and then to put such tariff cuts into effect in U.S. law via tariff-proclamation authority. This period ended as the post-war economic order began to break down, and various nations and blocs were challenging U.S. economic dominance. This led to the fourth regime from 1967 to 1975, when there was no delegated authority.

The fifth regime, dating from the mid 1970s to 2008, is the Fast Track period. What *on paper* entailed greater congressional involvement

---

8. RMSN, 1994.

(relative to the 1934-67 system of unilateral executive-branch tariff-proclamation authority), *in practice* provided the executive greater control over U.S. trade and non-trade policies than the country had ever seen. Fast Track, originally justified as a way to enhance U.S. competitiveness in the face of European and Japanese competition, instead coincided with a period of record-breaking U.S. trade deficits and deindustrialization. As noted, the mechanism also facilitated passage of pacts that delved deeply into domestic non-trade congressional and subfederal jurisdiction.

In the late 1980s, Congress sought to substantially amend the Fast Track mechanism, with reforms aimed at inserting a greater congressional role in the formative aspects of trade agreements. However, the effectiveness of these changes subsequently proved disappointing when the addition of congressional negotiating objectives – which were non-binding, a key feature and problem with Fast Track – produced the controversial NAFTA and WTO.

By the mid 1990s, wide bipartisan support for Fast Track had evaporated. The Clinton administration's attempt to obtain a delegation of Fast Track authority was rejected on the House floor in 1998 by 71 Republicans and 177 Democrats. The final delegation of Fast Track authority only passed by a one-vote margin in the middle of the night in 2002 after two years of effort by the George W. Bush administration. After Fast Track authority expired in 2007, Congress rebuffed President Bush's attempts to obtain additional Fast Track authority in 2008. The Obama administration did not seek a grant of the extraordinary authority from Congress in its first term.

The narrative that emerged from our research is one of Congress modifying the processes for coordinating with the executive branch regarding trade-agreement negotiations as external circumstances changed. As the United States has refined its approach to trade and global economic integration many times over, Congress has updated how it authorizes the executive branch to conduct negotiations on agreements that set the trade policies under Congress' constitutional authority. This book provides details of the various congressional efforts to modify Fast Track from 1988 on. And, the epilogue, includes some recent proposals to replace Fast Track with a new mechanism designed to reflect better the realities of the scope of subject matter now included in trade agreement negotiations. One such proposal, outlined in the 111th Congress in the Trade Reform Accountability Development and Employment (TRADE) Act, obtained 135 bipartisan House cosponsors. The epilogue also reviews President Obama's 2008 campaign commitments in this area.

Our tour through the history of U.S. trade agreement power sharing between Congress and the executive branch leads to the conclusion that it is possible to formulate a new mechanism to harvest the benefits of trade expansion without undermining key precepts of U.S. democracy such as checks and balances and federalism. It is also possible to protect and maintain the policy space that Congress and state legislatures need to meet the challenges now facing the nation. Enacting such an updated process will require Congress to consider *what* mechanism is appropriate to today's economic and governance realities, rather than simply *whether* to delegate more Fast Track authority when it is next requested by a U.S. president.

Finally, a methodological note. From 2005 to 2009, Public Citizen staff conducted in-depth research on the history of Congress' delegation of its constitutional trade authority and the origins of Fast Track. We were surprised at the dearth of scholarly material on the topic. Historians and presidential biographers have tended to overlook the battles over Fast Track and other previous trade-authority delegation procedures, or to downplay their divisiveness. Trade lawyers often ignored the politics and economics of trade-agreement policy. Political scientists, economists and sociologists looked at the history of trade-agreement authority delegation as little more than a stand-in for debates about "protectionism."

These perspectives obscure crucial questions about the mechanism's concentration of power within the executive branch, the effect of process on the premise and practice of federalism, and the related expansion of "trade" negotiations into wide swaths of non-trade policy – a feature that makes the Fast Track mechanism and era unique. Moreover, to the extent that the preexisting scholarly work touched on the trade authority issue, it relied almost entirely on secondary sources. When we began checking original sources, we found important aspects of the existing scholarly work to be incomplete, inaccurate or inadequately referenced. This was especially the case with regard to descriptions of how past delegation systems operated and to characterizations of the views of the opponents of such delegation mechanisms. It is important to note that many of these opponents presciently predicted the very governance and federalism issues that today's expansive trade agreements raise.

In order to understand this history more clearly, we spent months in the stacks of the Library of Congress piecing together the facts from the pre-electronic record era. We reviewed hundreds of volumes of 18th, 19th and early 20th Century U.S. statutes and the *Congressional Record,* dozens of committee reports and decades of newspaper prints. Hopefully, this book provides a more complete, accurate and interdisciplinary account of a timeless constitutional issue that will foster further study and theoretical work, as well as facilitate a more historically-informed discussion of this matter by Congress when a U.S. president next requests trade authority.

This book has two companion pieces: one that reviews the major economic outcomes of the international commercial agreements established under Fast Track[9], and another that compares the treatment of subfederal governments and their policy space under the U.S. trade-agreement policymaking process to that of other federal systems internationally, including those of Canada and Belgium.[10] Public Citizen recognizes the generous support of the Alfred P. Sloan Foundation in making possible the research and publication of this material.

9. Public Citizen, updated version 2013.
10. Bottari and Wallach, 2008.

An important factor leading to the American Revolution was colonists' fury about the trade policies imposed on them by Great Britain's King George. The Boston Tea Party, protesting the British tea monopoly and tariff policy, is depicted above.

Regime I. U.S. Trade Agreement Policymaking for the First 100 Years

America's founding fathers were acutely aware of the perils of concentrated power in trade policymaking. "No taxation without representation" was the rallying cry of the Boston colonists, including some of the founders themselves. Their Boston Tea Party was a turning point in the independence movement. The tax in question, however, was a tariff on tea, imported for sale in the colonies and initially imposed by King George to pay off his French war debts. In December 1773, Sam Adams, later a signatory of the new Constitution, led his fellow Sons of Liberty onto ships that had broken a colonial tea boycott organized in response to the tariff, and threw the ships' cargo into the Boston Harbor.[11]

In designing the Constitution, America's founding fathers created a clear separation of powers regarding trade policymaking. They sought thereby to avoid two problems which they had directly experienced:

---

11. Labaree, 1979.

13

an imperial ruler susceptible to foreign intrigues who bartered away the interests of the country and its citizens, and a states-dominated Articles of Confederation where each state had the power to impose tariffs on each other's products. Chief Justice John Marshall later remarked that nothing "contributed more to that general revolution which introduced the present system, than the deep and general conviction that commerce ought to be regulated by Congress."[12] As outlined in Article I, Section 8 of the U.S. Constitution, the body closest to the people was given the exclusive authority "to regulate commerce with foreign nations" and "lay and collect taxes [and] duties." This authority ensured a federally uniform trade policy. Meanwhile, the executive branch was given the authority to negotiate treaties on behalf of the United States in Article II, Section 2.

This system was buttressed by the wise logic of Alexander Hamilton, who wrote about the power over treaties (which was at the time the sole form of trade pacts) in *The Federalist No. 75*. He analyzed the relationship of trade to the balance of power between the executive and legislative branches of government thus:

> "The power of making treaties is, plainly, neither the one nor the other. It relates neither to the execution of the subsisting laws, nor to the enaction of new ones; and still less to an exertion of the common strength. Its objects are CONTRACTS with foreign nations, which have the force of law, but derive it from the obligations of good faith. They are not rules prescribed by the sovereign to the subject, but agreements between sovereign and sovereign. The power in question seems therefore to form a distinct department, and to belong, properly, neither to the legislative nor to the executive. The qualities elsewhere detailed as indispensable in the management of foreign negotiations, point out the Executive as the most fit agent in those transactions; while the vast importance of the trust, and the operation of treaties as laws, plead strongly for the participation of the whole or a portion of the legislative body in the office of making them... The history of human

---

12. *Brown v. Maryland*, 25 U.S. 12 Wheat. 419 (1827).

conduct does not warrant that exalted opinion of human virtue which would make it wise in a nation to commit interests of so delicate and momentous a kind, as those which concern its intercourse with the rest of the world, to the sole disposal of a magistrate created and circumstanced as would be a President of the United States."

In the words of one trade historian, "this complex system of checks and balances guarded the nation against human error and foreign corruption."[13] The divided power system provided an open political 'space' for elaborating and debating different views about the best mode of development for the new American nation. While heads of state like Thomas Jefferson embraced the idea of an economy that would export agriculture to Europe and import manufactured goods, congressional leaders like Henry Clay of Kentucky could advocate from their congressional perch for an "American system" of infant-industry protection and government investments to diversify the American economy. Because the Constitution gave Clay and his congressional colleagues the ultimate authority to approve trade policies, but required the president to conduct negotiations, neither branch could control the process.

Tariff acts were the primary means of implementing policy regarding the terms of trade between the United States and other nations. From 1789 until 1890, Congress enacted 16 major tariff acts, most of which increased rates, but nearly a third of which decreased them.[14] Each of these bills consisted of a long list of duties for customs officials to charge on imports, irrespective of originating country. The "single-column" tariff schedule greatly frustrated the executive branch, which sought the use of country-differentiated tariff tools in its diplomatic toolbox.

In 1790-93, then-Secretary of State Jefferson advocated for the executive branch to dangle both carrots (reciprocal tariff reductions) and sticks (retaliatory sanctions) in front of Europe to gain better treatment for American traders. However, the idea of providing the

---

13. Eckes, 1995, at 10.
14. The years of passage were 1789, 1790, 1792, 1804, 1816, 1824, 1828, *1832*, *1833*, 1842, *1846*, *1857*, 1861, *1872*, 1875, and 1883. Italicized years indicate tariff acts that reduced duties.

executive branch with such a broad delegation of Congress' constitutional tariff-setting authority – and such a high degree of discretion about tariff rates and treatment of specific countries – did not gain traction in Congress for another 100 years.

That does not mean that the executive did not *try* to sign trade treaties. However, in doing so, presidents were required to surmount two constitutional hurdles. First, they were required to use the constitutional treaty process (Senate advice and consent by two-thirds vote) to approve the agreements in question. Second, once an agreement was so approved, both chambers had to pass legislation making the treaty-required changes to U.S. tariff rates.[15] A comprehensive review of U.S. statute books did not yield a single bilateral tariff-lowering treaty adopted through this two-step process until 1854. (There were, however, several instances of Congress passing embargoes on certain nations' goods at wartime, but then allowing the executive unilaterally to remove the embargo once hostilities ceased or diminished, a procedure that was upheld by the Supreme Court in *Aurora v. the United States* in 1813.)

Congress generally viewed executive trade treaties as infringing on Congress' constitutional authority to set tariff rates. In 1844, 1855 and 1859, the executive branch negotiated reciprocal trade deals with Prussia, Hawaii and Mexico that would have applied tariffs to these countries' products that were lower than the single-rate duty established by Congress. In the first two instances, the executive branch wrote specific tariff changes into the treaties, while the Mexico treaty would have allowed Congress to select specific items for tariff reductions from a list pre-selected by the U.S. and Mexican executives. In each of these instances, Congress voted down the treaties. On the Prussia treaty, historian Alfred Eckes writes:

> "On June 14, 1844, the Senate Foreign Relations Committee released a critical report advising against ratification. It held that 'the control of trade and the function of taxing belong, without abridgement or participation, to Congress.' Representatives

---

15. Shapiro, 2006, at 89-92.

of the people 'may better discern what true policy prescribes and rejects, than is within the competence of the Executive department.' The appropriate function of the executive, the committee said, was 'to follow, not to lead; to fulfill, not to ordain, the law…, not to go forward with [a] too ambitious enterprise." [The Senate report] counsel[ed] rejection on constitutional grounds."[16]

Congress shelved various other executive attempts at trade treaties in this period. One such instance was a later 1867 Hawaii pact that Congress never considered in a legislative agenda dominated by Southern Reconstruction efforts. In the face of congressional opposition, the executive abandoned still other tariff-cutting trade pacts, including a tariff reciprocity pact with Canada that the James Polk administration had attempted to pass via normal (non-treaty) legislative procedures in the 1840s.[17]

There were only a few exceptions to Congress' general antipathy to executive trade pacts during the first regime. One occurred when the executive negotiated a reciprocity treaty in 1854 with Canada – signed on June 5 – that eliminated duties on 28 items (mostly food and raw materials). The Senate gave its advice and consent to the treaty, the text of which specified that: "The present treaty shall take effect as soon as the law required to carry it into operation shall have been passed… by the Congress of the United States." Thus, in order to make the duty eliminations operational, Congress had to pass separate implementing legislation, which it did on August 5. Once these steps were completed, President Franklin Pierce ratified the treaty in September.[18]

Congress later abrogated the treaty in 1866, since Canada had angered Congress by *increasing* duties on other U.S. products during the period. At the time, Senator Justin Morrill (R-Vt.), chair of the Senate Finance Committee, declared that tariff reciprocity treaties are "a plain and palpable violation of the Constitution, which gives to the House of Representatives the sole power to originate revenue

---

16. Eckes, 1995, at 65.
17. USITC, 1919.
18. Reciprocity Treaty with Great Britain, Proclamation by President Franklin Pierce, June 5, 1854, Articles 3 and 5; Public Law 33-144.

bills."[19] (Since America's early years, the Senate Finance and House Ways & Means committees have played a leading role in trade policy, given tariffs are considered an instrument of tax policy, and these committees have jurisdiction over such revenue measures. Because of this jurisdictional distinction, the committees are often called trade-policy "gatekeepers.")

In another exceptional move, the Senate gave its advice and consent to – and Congress passed implementing legislation for – an 1875 Hawaii tariff-reciprocity treaty negotiated by the Ulysses Grant administration. This surprised some, since the Senate had failed to give its advice and consent to yet another Canadian tariff reciprocity treaty the year before. However, the pro-tariff Republican *Chicago Daily Tribune* (now known simply as the *Chicago Tribune*) editorialized that one could be *for* the Hawaii pact and still *against* reciprocity more generally, since the former "affects injuriously very few, if any, vested interests in this country," and, "It is better to have reciprocal free trade with the Sandwich Islands [Hawaii] than to annex them." (Policymakers considered annexation the only alternative policy, given U.S. military interests in securing the Pacific.[20] Hawaii became a U.S. territory in 1900, an arrangement that supplanted the reciprocity treaty.)

From a purely economic point of view, the almost total lack of U.S. trade pacts during America's first 100 years did not prove detrimental: real per capita income grew 389 percent, or an annual average of 4 percent.[21] During the nation's first century, presidents and legislators of all political parties tended to agree on the constitutional basis for congressional control over trade policy, even when they disagreed on trade policies and economics *per se*. (Democrats tended to favor tariffs for revenue only, while Republicans tended to favor tariffs in order to develop infant industries.) Nevertheless, the congressionally controlled system began to unravel as U.S. global ambitions expanded, and the executive branch increasingly demanded it be granted trade tools to reward allies and punish enemies in the context of broader foreign-policy goals.

19. Eckes, 1995, at 68.
20. CDT, 1875.
21. Johnston and Williamson, 2008.

Regime II. Baby Steps Towards Delegated Tariff Authority, 1890-1934

a. Initial Delegation of Tariff Authority Raises Supreme Court Challenge, 1890-97

The traditionally pro-tariff Republican Party initiated the shift away from congressional control over trade policy. In 1890, Republican President Benjamin Harrison and his secretary of state, James Blaine, tried to persuade Congress to grant the executive branch expanded discretion of tariff policy. Again, Senate Finance Committee Chair Morrill blocked the executive-branch intrusions, angering Blaine to the point where he smashed his silk hat in one of Morrill's hearings.[22]

Blaine was able to get around Morrill by developing a partnership with the traditionally pro-tariff Ways & Means Chair William McKinley. The outcome of their joint effort was the 1890 McKinley Tariff Act, passed by Congress and signed into law in that year. The bill cleverly introduced the notion of delegated authority. It employed Congress' trade authority to raise tariffs on wool and other products but eliminate (via statute) duties on sugar, molasses, tea, coffee and hides. Meanwhile, it authorized the executive to *re-impose* such eliminated tariffs on countries that exported these products and treated U.S. exports in a "reciprocally unequal and unreasonable" fashion, *"with a view to secure reciprocal trade"* with said countries [italics added].[23] The delegation of tariff authority did not have a phase-out date. In effect, it allowed the Harrison administration to threaten to proclaim duty increases as a way of bringing foreign nations to the bargaining table. Congress did not have to vote on any trade pacts that resulted from these negotiations, since the intention was only to get other countries to lower *their* tariffs on U.S. exports.

Democrats assailed the measure, which they saw as a behind-the-scenes, inter-branch deal within the Republican Party. Rep. John F.

---

22. Eckes, 1995, at 71.
23. McKinley Tariff Act of 1890. 26 Stat.567; 51 Cong. Ch. 1244, § 3; H.R. 9416. House: 150-80; Senate: 33-27. Implemented October 6, 1890.

Andrew (D-Mass.) told the House: "It is free to say that such extraordinary powers as this amendment contemplates has never, in recent times, been given by a free people to the executive." [*sic*] Rep. Benton McMillin (D-Tenn.) declared, "the reciprocity provision of the bill was a cowardly surrender of the highest prerogative of the House. The bill gave the president power not exercised by the Czar of Russia."[24]

The Harrison administration rarely proclaimed any duty increases, but used the threat of doing so to negotiate 10 treaties that compelled other countries to lower their tariffs on select U.S. exports, in return for enjoying the statutorily established free rate on sugar and the other items.[25] These pacts also established a precedent of the executive branch framing requests for expanded authority around promises to penalize countries that denied access to U.S. exports.

In 1892, the Supreme Court was asked to rule on the constitutionality of the delegated tariff authority. This case involved a suit brought by an importer to obtain a refund of duties. The plaintiff, Marshall Field & Co., claimed that the duties it had been charged on its imported merchandise had been illegally exacted. Field filed against John Clark, the Chicago port's duty collector, to recover duties paid on woolen dress goods, woolen wearing apparel, and silk embroideries. The company was not an importer of sugar or other items contemplated for special treatment under the McKinley Act, but nonetheless maintained that the statutory rates on the items it *did* import (which had been raised by the act) were not legal.

Field argued that the McKinley Act (and its tariffs on wool and other items) did not have the force of law because (among other technical reasons) it unconstitutionally delegated congressional authority in the section on sugar powers. The majority opinion of the Supreme Court noted: "That Congress cannot delegate legislative power to the President is a principle universally recognized as vital to the integrity and

---

24. BDG, 1890.
25. The pacts were signed with Austria-Hungary (May 20, 1892), Brazil (April 1, 1891), the Dominican Republic (Sept. 1, 1891), El Salvador (Feb. 1, 1892), Germany (Feb. 1, 1892), Guatemala (May 30, 1892), Honduras (May 25, 1892), Nicaragua (March 12, 1892), Spain (for Cuba and Puerto Rico, Sept. 1, 1891), and the United Kingdom (for the British West Indies and British Guiana, Feb. 1, 1892). See NYT, 1901. Duty-free suspensions were declared on El Salvador, Colombia, Haiti, and Venezuela. See O'Halloran 1994.

maintenance of the system of government ordained by the Constitution." However, the Court majority decided that the Act's delegated authority "was not the making of law," but only allowing the executive branch to serve as "the mere agent of the law-making department."

Yet two justices, while agreeing with the majority ruling, dissented on the constitutionality of the delegation of tariff-proclamation authority. Chief Justice Melville Fuller and Associate Justice Joseph Lamar wrote that:

> "This [provision] certainly extends to the executive the exercise of those discretionary powers which the constitution has vested in the law-making ... department. It unquestionably vests in the president the power to regulate our commerce with all foreign nations which produce sugar, tea, coffee, molasses, hides, or any of such articles; and to impose revenue duties upon them for a length of time limited solely by his discretion, whenever he deems the revenue system or policy of any nation in which those articles are produced reciprocally unequal and unreasonable in its operation upon the products of this country. These features of this section are, in our opinion, in palpable violation of the Constitution of the United States, and serve to distinguish it from the legislative precedents which are relied upon to sustain it, as the practice of the government."[26]

After Ohio voters elected McKinley governor, and Democrat Grover Cleveland rode to the presidency on a low-tariff platform, Congress repealed the McKinley Act through the 1894 Wilson-Gorman Tariff Act. The law removed the executive's negotiating authority and abrogated the 10 Harrison treaties. It also modestly lowered duties overall, but was nonetheless full of duty increases designed to benefit certain industries (such as sugar).[27] (Cleveland was so embarrassed by the tariff increases that he refused to sign the bill into law. Nevertheless, because he also did not veto it, it became law after a lapse of time.)[28] The now Democratic-controlled Ways & Means Committee, in its

---

26. *Field v. Clark*, 143 U.S. 649, 692 (1892).
27. Wilson-Gorman Tariff Act of 1894, 53 Cong. Ch. 349.
28. IND, 1894.

report on the bill, assailed the previous Congress and administration: "We do not believe that Congress can rightly vest in the President of the United States any authority or power to impose or release taxes on our people by proclamation or otherwise, or to suspend or dispense with the operation of a law of Congress."[29]

The 1890's tariff acts were major political issues at the time. This political ad is critical of William McKinley, author of the 1890 McKinley Tariff Act. Later, as U.S. president, he signed the 1897 Dingley Tariff Act into law. In both roles, McKinley greatly expanded executive tariff discretion.

b. Second Delegation of Tariff-Cutting Authority, 1897-1909

The Democratic Party's control was short-lived. It lost both congressional chambers in the 1894 elections, followed by the presidency in the 1896 elections. Republicans again reinstated executive tariff-proclamation authority through the 1897 Dingley Tariff Act, which authorized now-President McKinley to proclaim unilaterally tariff reductions on wines and a few other specialty items. The authority

---

29. Eckes, 1995, at 74.

did not have a phase-out date. As with the 1890 McKinley Act, Congress limited both the items for which tariffs could be modified (for instance, sugar in 1890 and argols[30] in 1897) *and* the countries with which the executive could enter into trade negotiations (only countries that exported these items).[31] Eight European countries consented to the so-called "argol agreements".[32] Further, the Dingley Act contained provisions similar to the McKinley Act that authorized the executive branch to impose tariffs on various tropical items, but these provisions were never invoked or used to demand reciprocity treaties. Neither type of agreement required a further congressional vote.

The Dingley Act also authorized the president to negotiate with any country to secure reciprocal trade treaties that would cut tariffs up to 20 percent (and remove tariffs on certain natural resource products). The Act specified that these treaties *would* need the advice and consent of the Senate, and separate implementing legislation approved by congressional vote.[33] The McKinley administration finalized 11 such treaties, but leading senators opposed them, keeping them bottled up in the Senate Foreign Affairs Committee. Collectively, these were known as the Kasson Treaties, after John Kasson, the McKinley-appointed special commissioner for reciprocity negotiations.[34]

While none of the original 11 Kasson treaties gained congressional approval, President Theodore Roosevelt signed a reciprocity treaty with Cuba on Dec. 11, 1902 that lowered rates on Cuban imports by 20 percent. The Senate gave its advice and consent on March 19, 1903, but amended the treaty text to make clear that "This Convention shall not take effect until the same shall have been approved by the Congress." *Post facto,* Roosevelt decided to use the Kasson authority to get himself out of the mess. After a long fight – with opposition

---

30. Argols are a by-product of winemaking.
31. Dingley Tariff Act of 1897, 55 Cong. Ch. 11; 30 Stat. 151, Ch. 11, § 3; H.R. 379. House: 187-116. Senate: 40-30. Implemented July 24, 1897.
32. These included Spain, Bulgaria, France, Portugal, Germany, and Italy; along with more limited treaties for Great Britain and the Netherlands. See USITC, 1919.
33. Section 4 of Dingley Tariff Act.
34. Argentina (July 10, 1899); France (July 24, 1899); Nicaragua (Oct. 20, 1899); Dominican Republic (June 25, 1900); and Ecuador (July 10, 1900). Denmark also negotiated one for St. Croix (July 5, 1900). Finally, Great Britain negotiated five pacts (one each) for Barbados (June 16, 1899), British Guiana (July 18, 1899), Turks / Caicos (July 21, 1899), Jamaica (July 22, 1899), and Bermuda (July 24, 1899). See Holt, 1933, at 196.

from Democrats like Sen. Joseph Weldon Bailey (D-Texas), who called the act unconstitutional since the House had only been involved as an afterthought – on December 17, 1903, Roosevelt was able to get the Cuba trade deal implementing legislation through Congress based on foreign-policy arguments.[35] (Some form of Cuba tariff-reciprocity pact survived until the communist takeover in 1959.)

According to historian Alfred Eckes, some Washington officials were disheartened by the Kasson treaties experience, and by the successful completion of only three reciprocity treaties over 100 years (Canada 1854-1866, Hawaii 1875-1900, Cuba 1903-1959). Their prescription? Congress needed to delegate tariff-cutting negotiating authority to the executive, but not be allowed a vote on the negotiations' final outcome.[36]

c. Congress Provides Executive More Flexibility in Tariff Authority, 1909-1934

Until 1909, the U.S. tariff schedule was still officially single-column (i.e. one rate applied to all countries for each good) – even though Canada, Hawaii, and Cuba had enjoyed preferential rates under the three pacts described above. The 1909 Payne-Aldrich Act – passed by a Republican Congress – changed that, authorizing the president to proclaim unilaterally a "maximum tariff" for goods from countries that discriminated against U.S. exports. The authority did not have a phase-out date, and proclamations did not require further congressional votes. This maximum rate, which constituted the United States' first foray into a two-column tariff schedule, was equal to the normal (or "minimum") statutory rate plus 25 percent *ad valorem*.[37] (The William Taft administration never used this authority.) In addition, the Payne Act cancelled the eight argol treaties.

The only other major trade initiative of the Taft administration was to conduct secret trade negotiations with Canada. The U.S. President and Canadian Prime Minister planned to seek congressional and

---

35. NYT, 1903; WP, 1903; P.L. 58-1; Commercial Convention – Cuba Proclamation, Dec. 17, 1903.
36. Eckes, 1995, at 77.
37. Payne-Aldrich Act of 1909. Public Law 61-5; 36 Stat. 11, Ch. 6, sec. 1-2. H.R. 1438. House: 217-161. Senate: 45-34. Implemented August 6, 1909.

parliamentary approval, respectively, through normal legislative (i.e. non-treaty) procedures. Democrats in the U.S. Congress had teamed up with the Republican President and passed the bill, making boisterous but highly misleading floor statements to the effect that the act would allow U.S. annexation of the northern country. As a result, Canadian nationalists in the parliament rejected the pact's implementing legislation.[38]

The Woodrow Wilson administration came to office on a pledge to reduce tariffs, and was able to convince a Democratic-controlled Congress to do so through the 1913 Underwood-Simmons Act. The bill did away with the president's authority to penalize foreign countries through application of the maximum tariff, but it also authorized him to conduct reciprocal trade deals – "provided, however, that said trade agreements before becoming operative shall be submitted to the Congress of the United States for ratification or rejection."[39] The authority did not have a phase-out date. However, because the Underwood Act unilaterally reduced U.S. tariffs, foreign governments had little incentive to negotiate trade pacts with the United States, having received "something for nothing." No bilateral pacts were signed under the Underwood authority.

The general drift towards Congress' initial delegation of tariff authority to the executive branch continued in the next decade, as the GOP returned to power. Although it contained no specific tariff reciprocity authority, the 1922 Fordney-McCumber Tariff Act delegated a new authority to President Warren Harding and his successors. Under the act, the executive branch could raise or lower tariffs by proclamation to equalize the costs of production of articles produced in the United States and competitor countries. The authority did not have a phase-out date. It limited the rate alteration, however, to no more than 50 percent of the underlying statutory duty.[40] Congress did not have to vote on these reductions.

---

38. Eckes, 1995, at 83-84.
39. United States Revenue Act of October 3, 1913, Public Law 63-16; 38 Stat. 116, Ch. 16, sec. 4(a); H.R. 3321. House: 255-104. Senate: 44-37. Implemented October 4, 1913,
40. Fordney-McCumber Tariff of 1922. Public Law 67-318; 36 Stat 11, Ch. 356, sec. 315; H.R. 7456. Implemented September 22, 1922.

The Republican-controlled Congress supported their party's president in this proposal, but some Democrats bitterly attacked the proposal. The *New York Times* reported that Sen. Thomas Walsh (D-Mont.) "told the Senate the Constitution specifically reserved to Congress the power to lay and collect taxes and import duties, and Congress could not delegate this authority. He also attacked the flexible plan on the ground that no provision was made for judicial review of the president's action."[41]

Harding and his immediate successors did not craft reciprocity treaties that required Senate approval and congressional implementing legislation. Instead the administrations negotiated a series of over 40 executive agreements that established Most Favored Nation treatment for additional countries, granting those countries the same preferential tariff rates afforded by the United States to various other countries. By merely guaranteeing tariff treatment already codified in statute, the executive avoided having to ask Congress to change any underlying laws.[42]

The beginning of the Great Depression in the United States is associated with the stock market crash on October 29, 1929, known as Black Tuesday. One of Congress' responses was to pass the Smoot-Hawley Tariff Act, which went into effect on June 17, 1930. The Act returned the United States to 19th-century tariff levels.[43] Smoot-Hawley did not change the fundamental executive-legislative balance in any way from the 1922 Act. This is notable, because editorial boards and politicians still invoke the bill with contempt, if inaccuracy, whenever the suggestion is made to increase congressional involvement in trade policymaking.

In 1932, Sen. Cordell Hull (D-Tenn.) led an effort to give President Herbert Hoover the discretion to negotiate bilateral tariff-reduction pacts, subject to separate congressional approval. While both chambers passed the legislation, Hoover vetoed the bill, noting opposition to the

---

41. NYT, 1922.
42. WM, 1934, at 10. This was similar to practice in the pre-1890 period, when numerous presidents negotiated executive agreements and treaties to not discriminate against certain countries' imports *beyond* the duties mandated by statute.
43. Eckes, 1995, at 100-139.

congressional approval requirement, and it never became law.[44]

The Roaring Twenties produced new constitutional challenges to delegated presidential tariff authority. As it had in 1892, the Supreme Court again upheld the constitutionality of congressional delegation mechanisms. In *J. W. Hampton, Jr. & Co. v. United States*, the plaintiff imported barium dioxide into New York ports that the customs collector assessed at the dutiable rate of six cents per pound, which was two cents per pound more than that fixed by statute. The higher rate had been established by virtue of the presidential proclamation authority to equalize the costs of domestic and imported goods provided in the Fordney-McCumber Act. The company argued that Congress' delegation of constitutional tariff authority was unconstitutional, and thus did not have the force of law. In 1928, the Supreme Court, affirming a lower-court decision, held that congressional delegation of tariff authority was constitutional. The court interpreted the Fordney-McCumber Act as empowering and directing the president to increase or decrease duties imposed by Congress. The Court reasoned that one of the core functions that the Constitution confers on Congress is the regulation of interstate commerce, yet noted that Congress does not attempt to manage interstate freight rates directly, a highly complex and rapidly changing task. Therefore, the Court concluded that delegation of setting specific tariffs rates to the executive under policies established by Congress should also be constitutional.[45]

Despite the expanded presidential trade authority during the 1890-1934 regime, the second major period of U.S. trade policymaking ended with high tariffs and relatively few trade agreements. The regime also saw an unusual shift in the politics of trade. Republican Congresses and executives under the Harrison, McKinley, Taft and Harding administrations – while favoring higher tariffs – took groundbreaking steps to expand executive discretion. Democrats – who favored lower tariffs – often argued in favor of the principle of congressional control, regularly raising concerns about the constitutional issues involved. The latter party passed legislation scraping back what they deemed

---

44. H.R. 6662. The House passed 214-182, and the Senate passed 42-30.
45. *J. W. Hampton, Jr. & Co. v. United States*, 276 U.S. 394 (1928). For an account of this case and the ongoing debate around the nondelegation doctrine, see Wertkin, 2002.

to be inappropriate executive branch overreach into congressional constitutional authority in 1894 and 1913.

Notably, the period also saw the emergence of radical views on altering the constitutional trade checks and balances. Rep. Martin Ansorge (R-N.Y.) proposed a constitutional amendment to outsource trade policy permanently from Congress to a non-partisan board.[46] Ansorge only served one term in Congress. Nevertheless, the notion gained serious consideration in the subsequent trade-policy regime from 1934-1967.

---

46. NYT, 1922.

Regime III. Executive Proclamation of Tariffs, 1934-1967

a. Reciprocal Trade Agreements Act Dramatically Increases Executive Trade Authority, 1934-45

A new and sweeping form of delegated authority was established in the Trade Agreement Expansion Act of 1934, more commonly known as the Reciprocal Trade Agreements Act (RTAA). The legislation authorized the executive branch to enter into trade agreements that modified tariffs and other import restrictions (such as quotas), and unilaterally proclaim tariff increases or decreases within a 50 percent band for pact partners' U.S. exports. While duty negotiations would proceed on an item-by-item basis, the legislation set no limit on the types of goods for which duties could be revised, unlike many past congressional delegations. The proposed authority also left to the executive's discretion whether or not to extend benefits negotiated bilaterally to *all* other countries on a most-favored nation basis, or only to *specific* countries that engaged in U.S. negotiations.[47]

The act – an amendment to Smoot-Hawley that the Franklin Roosevelt administration justified as "emergency" legislation – provided for no subsequent congressional votes on the resulting agreements, or congressional right of appeal on executive-branch decisions. The act specified no negotiating objectives or countries with which to negotiate. The only minimal requirement was for "reasonable public notice of the intention to negotiate an agreement," and for presidential consultation with relevant governmental agencies. But in at least one respect, the administration's depiction of the bill as emergency legislation was backed up on paper: the authority was to only last for three years, and agreements that it established were subject to termination upon its expiration.[48] However, in practice, this new delegated authority and the agreements it established were extended every few years for a generation. In fact, RTAA's sweeping authority became a precedent

---

47. WM, 1934, at 10.
48. Trade Agreement Expansion Act of 1934. Public Law 73-316; 48 Stat. 943; H.R. 8687. On March 29, the House approved H.R. 8687 by 271-110 (D: 269-11; R: 2-99). On June 4, the Senate approved the measure 56-33 (D: 51-5; R: 5-28).

for future, increasingly expansive delegations. In his book on Fast Track, Hal Shapiro, a former associate general counsel in the Office of the U.S. Trade Representative (USTR), notes how the RTAA "was a major departure in that it effectively 'pre-approved' presidential authority to negotiate international trade agreements."[49] Congress had previously delegated to the executive both tariff-proclamation authority (for certain goods within certain bands) and limited authority to negotiate trade agreements that did not require congressional approval. But the RTAA – which included authority for the president also to change non-tariff items like quotas without a congressional vote – nonetheless significantly expanded presidential power.

What was the purpose of this new delegation? The RTAA divided opinion even within the Roosevelt administration. One faction held that the authority should be used primarily to ink bilateral agreements in order to stimulate exports and thus national income. Others maintained that the purpose was to lower tariffs unilaterally so as to increase imports, because the United States had *too high* of a trade surplus at the time.[50]

Such debates were beside the point to Roosevelt's secretary of state, former Democratic senator Cordell Hull. His outlook was as simplistic and unsubstantiated as it was infectious: low tariffs equal peace, and high tariffs equal war. Hull had spent years in Congress advocating for trade liberalization and greater executive authority. When Hull testified before the House Ways & Means Committee, he employed every conceivable rationale for the new authority: it was an essential part of the president's domestic recovery plan; a help to poor people abroad; and a way to put the U.S. executive on equal footing with heads of state in parliamentary systems (who had total tariff authority). He also admitted that the authority went beyond just tariffs, to encompass quotas and even possibly product-safety standards. He refused to speak in detail about how he planned to use the authority, citing a desire to avoid broadcasting U.S. negotiating positions to foreign governments. In an exchange with Rep. Allen Treadway (R-Mass.),

49. Shapiro, 2006, at 10.
50. Schlesinger, 1958, at 254-260.

30

Hull made clear that he thought the constitutionality of the measure was beside the point:

> Treadway: *Under the Constitution, article 1, section 7, all bills for raising revenue shall originate in the House of Representatives; but the Senate may propose or concur with amendments as on other bills. Are we in any way violating that provision of the Constitution in setting up a law such as we have before us?*

> Hull: *This bill is originating in the House, is it not? So far as I am individually concerned, I think I have in mind all of these phases, but at the same time I am literally moved, driven and kicked into another line of thinking, which relates to 30 million unemployed people in the world who cannot furnish food or clothing to their people because international trade has been choked down...*

> Treadway: *If those 30 million people scattered throughout the world and their families are a first consideration, should not that clause of the Constitution be amended in order to take care of the 30 million people and not to violate the Constitution directly by legislative action?*

> Hull: *That is what they said to Abraham Lincoln when he had to suspend one or two phases for the time being... Very few democratic forms of government are left – mighty few. My observation after rather careful investigation has been that the mainspring or the moving influence of those revolutions has been people out of work... We are not going to fall into that soon, but you could easily become victims of those things in other parts of the world, and for that reason I would invoke your attention long enough to deal with this emergency situation...*

Treadway: *Assuming that to be true, and of course it is all open to debate... is the measure you are presenting to us today constitutional?*

Hull: *My opinion is that it is up to the Congress to cooperate with another coordinate branch of the Government to determine, first, whether this real exigency, present and prospective, does exist, and whether it is of such magnitude in its effect upon our country as would justify either branch of Congress or both in giving authority to the executive department in advance to perform certain functions which would ordinarily be reviewed by one branch of the legislative department.*[51]

Hull and administration allies like Rep. Samuel Hill (D-Wash.) also argued that the Supreme Court was likely to uphold the constitutionality of the delegation, since the previous trade regime's flexible tariff provisions had been upheld as constitutional. In a later hearing, Hill argued that the record of congressional approval of only three reciprocity treaties:

"show[s] the inefficiency of that kind of treaty making... whereas Executive agreements have produced a substantial number of reciprocal trade agreements. It seems to me in the fact of the history of this country upon that subject that to advocate a resort to the ordinary treaty-making power of the President for the purpose of effecting trade agreements or trade relationships, we must concede it simply an argument that that does not get us anywhere so far as effective progress is concerned toward improving our trade relationships with foreign countries."[52]

Hull established an inter-agency Committee on Trade Agreements housed in the State Department that was tasked with promoting what he saw as U.S. *foreign-policy* interests by reducing U.S. tariffs.

---

51. WM, 1934, at 15-18.
52. WM, 1934, at 407-408.

The arrangement was so far removed from the days of congressional control of trade policy that Roosevelt and successor administrations would not even reveal the identity of the committee's members to the public. Rep. Daniel Reed (R-N.Y.) made a prescient remark during RTAA's floor debate that "such power, if granted, will place the life and death of every industry at the mercy of the 'brain trust'."[53] These Committee officials saw their role as picking economic winners and losers, and even coded industries based on their perceived export competitiveness.[54] Congress renewed the RTAA in 1937, 1940, 1943 and 1945, each for a three-year term.[55] Roosevelt and later Truman proclaimed 40 bilateral deals with 24 countries between 1935 and 1946, dealing mostly with tariffs, but also occasionally with quotas and customs regulations.[56]

b. Rise of the GATT, 1945-51

A major challenge to the RTAA's expanded executive trade authority came when the Truman administration interpreted it as allowing the multilateral trade negotiations that established the General Agreement on Tariffs and Trade (GATT). The 1944 Bretton Woods Conference originally envisioned the creation of three new institutions to regulate postwar global economic relations: the International Monetary Fund (IMF), the International Bank for Reconstruction and Development (the World Bank) and an International Trade Organization (ITO).

---

53. Rep. Daniel Reed (R-N.Y.), *Congressional Record*, 78, March 27, 1934, at 5533.
54. Eckes, 1995, at 94-177.
55. The 1937 Act passed the House 281-92 (D: 278-11; R: 3-81) and the Senate 56-23 (D: 56-9; R: 0-14). The 1940 Act passed the House 217-166 (D: 212-20; R: 5-146) and the Senate 41-35 (D: 41-15; R: 0-20). The 1943 Act passed the House 340-63 (D: 212-20; R: 145-52) and the Senate 59-22 (D: 41-8; R: 8-14). The 1945 Act passed the House 238-152 (D: 205-12; R: 33-140) and the Senate 53-21 (D: 38-5; R: 15-16).
56. Trade agreements concluded under RTAA include: Argentina (Oct. 14, 1941), Belgium-Luxembourg (Feb. 27, 1935), Brazil (Feb. 2, 1935, June 30, 1948), Canada (Nov. 15, 1935, Nov. 30, 1939, Dec. 30, 1939, Nov. 30, 1940, Dec. 13, 1940, Dec. 22, 1941), Colombia (Sept. 13, 1935), Costa Rica (Nov. 28, 1936), Cuba (Aug. 24, 1935, Dec. 18, 1939, Dec. 23, 1941), Ecuador (March 2, 1942), El Salvador (Feb. 19, 1937), Finland (May 18, 1936), Guatemala (April 24, 1936), Haiti (March 28, 1935, Feb. 16-19, 1942, April 25, 1942), Honduras (Dec. 18, 1935), Iran (April 8, 1943), Netherlands (Dec. 20, 1935), Nicaragua (March 11, 1936, Feb. 8, 1938), Paraguay (Sept. 12, 1946), Peru (May 7, 1942), Sweden (May 25, 1935), Switzerland (Jan. 7, 1936, Nov. 28, 1940), Turkey (April 1, 1939, April 14-22, 1944), United Kingdom (Nov. 17, 1938), Uruguay (July 21, 1942), and Venezuela (Nov. 6, 1939, Dec. 12, 1939, Dec. 28, 1940, Dec. 26, 1941).

However, many in Congress were opposed to the ITO. Some in Congress raised concerns that, while the administration agreed to submit U.S. membership in the ITO to a treaty vote, Congress would have no vote on the nearly two-dozen reciprocal trade agreements that prospective ITO member countries had negotiated. The RTAA *did* allow the executive branch to enter unilaterally into such tariff-cutting agreements. But the practical implications of the RTAA's delegation of power was revealed dramatically by the prospect of the ITO establishing – in one fell swoop – a comparable number of new trade agreements as had been established in the previous 12 years.

Others in Congress opposed the ITO on the grounds that establishing a global commerce agency would undermine U.S. sovereignty. On April 7, 1947, several House members engaged in an impassioned colloquy on the topic:

> Rep. Noah Mason (R-Ill.): *This International Trade Organization, in effect, would be an international super state. It would take away from the American people control of American production... [it] would mean to transfer our governmental powers to a world economic authority.... We must halt this vicious plan for an International Trade Organization before it goes too far or it will be the undoing of everything that we have built up and developed under our Constitution...*

> Rep. Cliff Clevenger (R-Ohio): *As we sit in this committee, our Democratic friends are in a quandary. They have got their feet all tangled up and their eyes dim with the mist of the halo that has been around the head of Cordell Hull for so many years. They do not know where they are going... It is time that somebody rub a little Americanism on this party that rules the other end of [Pennsylvania] Avenue in order to get them to think America and work for America and protect America...*

> Rep. Thomas Owens (R-Ill.): *Aside from the fact that the executive department has emergency powers during wartime,*

is there any question in the gentleman's mind but that this Congress has the right to make laws and have the executive department enforce them, and that it is about time that we begin to do that in order to save our national policy?

Mason: *Of course, for 150 years, that was true, but that has not been true during the last 16 years, because not only has the judiciary department interpreted the laws and said what the Congress should have put in, whether they put it in or not, but our executive departments have been themselves interpreting the laws to suit themselves, and the business of the Congress today is quite largely the vetoing of department rulings which misinterpret the laws, and even vetoing some of the rulings of the Supreme Court on the laws that we have passed…*

Rep. John Rankin (D-Mo.): *I understood that… whatever agreements were made [in Geneva] should come back to the Congress for ratification; at least, to the Senate…*

Mason: *[The administration] said he would submit that to the Senate for approval before it would go into effect. He said, however, that as to the 18 reciprocal trade agreements which they expect to put into effect before this International Trade Organization is set up, they, of course, would not go to the Senate.[57]*

Indeed, by late 1947, the 23 countries that had originally engaged in GATT negotiations had already agreed to many tariff concessions. These were made on an item-by-item, bilateral, request-offer basis, and then generalized on a most-favored nation basis to the entire group. Truman, anxious to lock in these agreements, invoked the RTAA to proclaim the "provisional application" of the GATT to the United States in October 1947, which enshrined the tariff changes into law.[58] On March 24, 1948, Truman's Assistant Secretary of State William Clayton signed the ITO's draft charter, which would go into effect subject to congressional approval. On April 28, 1949, the Truman

---

57. *Congressional Record*, 93, April 7, 1947, at 3182-3184.
58. T.I.A.S. 1700, Vol. 1, Oct. 30, 1947; Jackson, 1967.

administration notified Congress it would submit the ITO for a Senate treaty vote, but then formally abandoned the effort in 1951 in the face of unbending congressional opposition.[59]

Members of Congress were irate at the executive branch's GATT maneuvering, as evidenced by comments at a Senate Finance Committee hearing from 1949:

> Sen. Eugene Millikin (R-Colo.): *Would the provisions of this article or any other part of GATT impose upon the Federal Government any duties to do anything as to local State laws or movements, which are intended to promote State products, such as 'Buy Georgia Peaches,' 'Buy Colorado Cantaloupes,' state advertising campaigns out of public funds to promote those local buying campaigns?*
>
> Winthrop Brown (State Department Official): *No, sir.*
>
> Millikin: *Is there anything in this agreement any place that imposes any obligation on the Federal Government to stop anything of that sort?*
>
> Brown: *I don't think so sir.*
>
> Millikin: *Is there any question about it?*
>
> Brown: *No, I don't know of anything.*[60]

Millikin and Brown had another face-off in March 1951:

> Millikin: *You are unwilling then to present the whole of GATT to Congress so that it might not only compare GATT against existing laws, but also against the Constitution? … What about the future laws of Congress?*
>
> Brown: *The answer to that question is that if the Congress should pass legislation in the future that was inconsistent with the GATT, they would put the United States in the position of violating the GATT.*

---

59. SF, 1951, at 1137, and 1143-44.
60. Quoted in Jackson, 1967, at 304.

Millikin: *And you feel that the President is warranted in making future executive agreements which in themselves might conflict with future laws of Congress?*

Brown: *That has been the situation with respect to all of our trade agreements since the beginning, Senator.*[61]

In 1947, Sen. Hugh Butler (R-Neb.) summed up the views of many when he said:

> "I think it is fair to say that it was not contemplated when this act was passed that it would be used as the vehicle for a general revision of our entire tariff system... the State Department has tried to commit us permanently to a reversal of our long-standing policies by putting this agreement through during a temporary period of world shortages. We may not realize fully what has happened to us for some little time... Present authority to negotiate these treaties under the Trade Agreements Act will expire next year. I believe the Congress will scrutinize very, very carefully any request for an extension."[62]

c. Congress Begins to Reassert Its Constitutional Trade Authority, 1948-1962

Butler's prediction came true. Republicans took over both chambers in the 1947 election on a pledge to rein in Truman. The following year, Congress enacted its first major RTAA revision, extending the authority for only a single year, rather than the customary three years. The 1948 RTAA introduced the rather modest notion that Congress and the trade gatekeeper committees (Senate Finance and House Ways & Means) would have to receive copies of any trade agreement that threatened "serious injury" to domestic industries within 30 days of entering into the pact. (This was known as the "peril-point" provision.[63]) In the House, 98 percent of Republicans supported the bill, and 90 percent of Democrats opposed – a total inversion of the pattern from previous RTAA extensions.

---

61. SF, 1951, at 1170.
62. Sen. Hugh Butler (R-Neb.), *Congressional Record*, 93, Nov. 20, 1947, at 10675.
63. Public Law 80-972. The 1948 Act passed the House 234-147 (D: 16-142; R: 218-5) and the Senate 70-18 (D: 23-17; R: 47-1).

The Republican resurgence was short-lived: Democrats retook both chambers later that year. In 1949, Congress reestablished the RTAA authority for its standard three-year duration, and removed the peril-point language.[64] While Democrats continued to hold the majority in the next Congress, the Republican minority was able to reinsert and expand the injury provision, and limit the 1951 extension of the authority to two years. The new language allowed either congressional chamber or gatekeeper committee to request that the Commerce Department's U.S. Tariff Commission (now called the U.S. International Trade Commission)[65] investigate and report on any "serious injury" caused to U.S. industries under a trade agreement. If the commission made a recommendation to alter tariff rates to compensate for the injury, the executive was authorized to proclaim further duty changes. If he chose to ignore the commission's advice, the president would have to file a report with the gatekeeper committees explaining his decision.

Additionally, the 1951 legislation specified, "the enactment of this act shall not be construed to indicate approval or disapproval by the Congress of the Executive Agreement known as the General Agreement on Tariffs and Trade."[66] Similar clauses appeared in the 1953, 1955 and 1958 acts, and were one means Congress had of showing that, while it accepted the tariff reductions proclaimed by the executive, it did not accept or recognize the GATT agreement itself, which extended into policy realms beyond tariffs.[67] In an early foreshadowing of how enhanced executive authority implicated non-tariff policy, the Truman administration admitted that a dozen domestic laws would have to be changed if the United States were to move from "provisional" to non-provisional acceptance of the GATT.[68]

---

64. Public Law 81-307; 63 Stat. 697; H.R. 1211. Approved on September 26, 1949. It passed 318-69 in the House (D: 234-6; R: 84-63) and 62-19 in the Senate (D: 47-1; R: 15-18).

65. The U.S. Tariff Commission was established by Congress in 1916. The 1974 Fast Track bill changed its name to the U.S. International Trade Commission. The USITC describes itself as: "An independent federal agency determining import injury to U.S. industries in antidumping, countervailing duty, and global and China safeguard investigations; directing actions against unfair trade practices involving patent, trademark, and copyright infringement; supporting policymakers through economic analysis and research on the global competitiveness of U.S. industries; and maintaining the U.S. Harmonized Tariff Schedule." See http://www.usitc.gov/.

66. Section 10 of Public Law 82-50; 65 Stat. 72; H.R. 1612. Approved on June 16, 1951. It passed 225-168 (D: 42-163; R: 183-4) in the House. In the Senate, it passed 72-2 (D: 38-0; R: 34-2).

67. Jackson, Louis and Matsushita, 1982, at 344-345.

68. SF, 1951, at 1195-1199.

While Roosevelt, Truman and congressional Democrats had hitherto treated any congressional alterations to the RTAA as partisan affronts, the 1952 elections provided something of a wakeup call. Republican Dwight Eisenhower defeated Democrat Adlai Stevenson for the presidency, and the Grand Old Party took both chambers of Congress. Democrats were henceforth less resistant to modifying the underlying formula, and bipartisan majorities voted over the decade to substantially increase congressional involvement in trade policy. The 1953 RTAA created a commission appointed by the executive and Congress that would study foreign economic policy, including its constitutional implications.[69] In the 1955 RTAA, Congress increased the executive's congressional reporting requirements.[70]

The 1958 RTAA renewal was Congress' most significant reassertion of congressional trade prerogatives during the third regime. This act allowed Congress to force the president to proclaim tariff modifications recommended by the Tariff Commission if he had initially rejected their advice. The exact process was the following: within 60 days of receiving the commission report initially mandated by the 1951 act, if both the House and Senate adopted a concurrent resolution by a two-thirds vote in each chamber requiring the commission's advice to be implemented, Congress could override the president. The bill also specified the rules that Congress would follow in considering such resolutions, while noting that these could be changed as per the legislature's constitutional remit. Under the rules, any member of Congress could propose such a "disapproval resolution," which would be automatically reported to the gatekeeper committees, who would have 10 days to report it out. If they did not take action after that time, any member of Congress could make a highly privileged motion (no amendments, one hour of debate, and other expediting procedures) for the resolution to be immediately discharged and brought up for a floor vote.[71]

---

69. Public Law 83-215; 67 Stat. 472. H.R. 5495 was approved on August 7, 1953. It passed 363-34 (D: 183-9; R-179-25) in the House and on July 2, 1953, it passed by voice vote in the Senate.
70. Public Law 84-86; 69 Stat. 162. H.R. 1 was approved on June 21, 1955. It passed 347-54 (D: 297-18; R: 150-36) in the House and 75-13 (D: 37-6; 38-7) in the Senate.
71. Public Law 85-686; 72 Stat. 673. H.R. 12591 was approved on August 20, 1958. It passed 317-98 (D: 184-39; R 133-59) in the House and 72-18 (D: 40-6; R: 32-12) in the Senate.

The Bricker Amendment: Bipartisan Criticism of Executive Unilateralism Grows

During this period, congressional concern about executive-branch unilateralism was significant, and not limited to trade-agreement matters. A constitutional amendment known as the Bricker Amendment, which would have significantly limited executive authority in the international arena, came within one vote of Senate approval.

Since the 1890s, Congress had allowed the executive to sign certain executive agreements that impacted trade without subsequent congressional approval, such as the argol agreements. Executive agreements around non-trade issues dated back even further. But their usage was growing increasingly controversial, as international agreements like the United Nations and GATT seemed to be creating supranational forms of governance.

In 1951-52, Sen. John Bricker (R-Ohio) – with support from the American Bar Association –proposed a constitutional amendment that no treaty or executive agreement could be made: 1) with respect to, abridging, or prohibiting the free exercise of Americans' constitutional rights; 2) that vests in any international organization or in any foreign power any of the legislative, executive, or judicial powers vested by this Constitution in the Congress, the President, and in the courts of the United States; or 3) that alters or abridges the Constitution or U.S. federal or state laws unless, and then only to the extent that, Congress shall so provide by joint resolution.

The Bricker Amendment would have also forbade executive agreements made in lieu of treaties, and would require that any executive agreements terminate within a year after the president who made them had left office, unless the following president asked Congress for an extension. Although not specifically directed against Truman's GATT maneuvers, Bricker's floor statements from January 1952 made his thinking clear: "The General Agreement on Tariffs and Trade is an illegal executive agreement launched with the idea of greasing the way for the International Trade Organization. The ITO, in both treaty and joint resolution form, met a stone wall in Congress. GATT, its illegitimate forerunner, lingers on."[72]

---

72. Sen. John Bricker (R-Ohio), *Congressional Record*, 98, Jan. 23, 1952.

In 1953-54, after the Republicans took back Congress, Bricker introduced revised versions of his Constitutional amendment, which attracted broad bipartisan support. But, Senate Minority Leader Lyndon Johnson – perhaps thinking about the executive-power question in the context of his own presidential aspirations – teamed up with Eisenhower to kill the amendment. On February 26, 1954, a watered down version of the Bricker Amendment authored by Sen. Walter George (D-Ga.) fell one vote short of the needed two-thirds supermajority, and thus died.[73] Despite growing bipartisan concerns about executive-branch unilateralism in the international arena, Truman and Eisenhower continued to rely on GATT's "provisional application," even as GATT contracting parties completed five rounds of GATT negotiations and U.S. administrations proclaimed the resulting tariff changes into U.S. law.

d. Yet Another Congressional-Executive Trade Authority Showdown, 1962-67

John F. Kennedy came to the presidency promising an overhaul of U.S. trade policy, stating that the 1934 RTAA model "must not simply be renewed, it must be replaced." He argued that this was necessary to meet the challenges of new developments on the trade horizon, such as the "need for us to maintain a balance of trade in our favor" by reducing European tariffs.[74] In practice, the 1962 Trade Expansion Act (TEA) did not represent a huge change in the RTAA's executive-legislative relationship. It added provisions that required the president to accredit a member of each party from each chamber to go on negotiating teams, and to send copies of completed agreements to Congress. Presidential tariff-proclamation authority was limited to increases or decreases within a 50 percent band. Certain duties could be totally eliminated, such as those already under 5 percent *ad valorem*, on tropical products, or on products where the U.S. dominated global markets. Moreover, the TEA extended tariff-proclamation authority from three to five years, through 1967, and created the Office of the Special Trade Representative (STR, later called the U.S. Trade Representative)

---

73. The debate is chronicled in Caro, 2002, at 527-541.
74. TIME, 1961.

to lead negotiating teams and serve as a broker between executive agencies.[75] Kennedy later placed the STR in the Executive Office of the President.

The 1962 act also pioneered the idea of buying congressional support for trade deals by attaching delegation authority to authorizations for a new program of trade adjustment assistance (TAA), which aided workers displaced by imports. The TAA legislative "sweetener" has since become standard political cover for members of Congress making difficult trade votes.[76] The administration tucked the new TAA program into the larger delegation proposal as a means to win labor support, as AFL-CIO President George Meany indicated when he told the Senate Finance Committee in 1962:

> "As you know, we in the AFL-CIO have consistently supported the various extensions of the Reciprocal Trade Act over the last 28 years. However, we agree with the administration that the time has now come for a fundamental revision, an updating and overhauling of this basic approach... Yet I gather from newspaper reports and other sources that trade adjustment assistance still remains one of the more controversial features of the program you are considering. This causes us the gravest concern. In our opinion, there is no question whatever that adjustment assistance is essential to the success of trade expansion. And as we have said before, it is indispensable to our support for the trade program as a whole."[77]

On June 28, the House approved the TEA by a margin of 299 to 125, and the Senate promptly followed.[78] After the Kennedy assassination the following year, countries participating in the sixth GATT negotiating round renamed it in Kennedy's honor. These negotiations were completed by President Lyndon Johnson, who used his TEA authority to make an executive proclamation enacting the round's sweeping tariff reductions.

---

75. Public Law 87-794 § 226 and 243.
76. Tucker, Wu and Prorok, 2005.
77. Testimony of George Meany. See SF, 1962, at 240-241.
78. Public Law 87-794 § 226 and 243. 76 Stat. 872. H.R. 11970 was approved on October 11, 1962. The House adopted it 256-91 (D: 178-34; R: 78-57) and, in the Senate, it passed 78-8 (D: 56-1; R: 22-7).

But Johnson made a number of legislative missteps that aroused congressional anger. First, he negotiated and signed an Automotive Products Agreement with Canada on January 15, 1965 without prior congressional authorization, congressional participation in the negotiations, or the required public hearings. The pact *eliminated* certain duties on cars and car parts, even though the TEA authority only allowed for reductions on these duties within the 50 percent band.

Sen. William Fulbright (D-Ark.) questioned why the executive was not asking for the Senate's advice and consent. In a letter to Secretary of State Dean Rusk, Fulbright noted: "An increasing number of members are under the impression that executive branch decisions whether to submit international agreements to the Senate for approval by two-thirds of its Members or to the Congress for a majority decision are based on expediency rather than the Constitution."

In response, the State Department wrote: "The United States-Canadian automotive agreement is bilateral and deals with the elimination of duties. It has been the regular practice for over 30 years to use the executive agreement-legislative authority procedure for agreements of this type. In the usual case, the legislative authority has been provided first and the executive agreement made later – as under the reciprocal trade legislation of 1934 and the Trade Expansion Act of 1962. However, it is equally within the constitutional powers of the President to make an executive agreement first, subject to the enactment of legislation and have the legislation follow."[79] Despite constitutional concerns, Congress passed the legislation, retroactively authorizing the negotiations and duty reductions, on October 21, 1965. Johnson proclaimed the duty reductions into effect the same day.[80]

Johnson made a second error in calculating Congress' tolerance for executive trade actions taken outside of delegated authority. In the Kennedy Round, he engaged in negotiations with GATT partners about changing U.S. antidumping law, and eliminating what was known as the American Selling Price (ASP), a method for valuating

---

79. Both letters were entered into committee records. WM, 1965, at 225-227.
80. Public Law 89-283; 79 Stat. 1016; H.R. 9042, passed Oct. 21, 1965.

certain foreign imports (of chemicals, for instance) based upon what they would have cost to produce in the United States. These were quintessential non-tariff (though trade-related) issues, and in June 1966, the Senate unanimously passed S. Con. Res. 100, which stated that the president should not engage in negotiations on matters for which he had no prior congressional authorization. Sen. Vance Hartke (D-Ind.) noted that "such substantive changes in our law amount to unauthorized legislation by an international agreement whose execution exceeds the mandate for these negotiations and usurps the legislative responsibilities of Congress."[81]

While Republicans had led the mid-century charge against executive concentration of trade power, Democrats – increasingly concerned with American workers' wellbeing under a global trading system – also joined the ranks of the critics of delegated trade authorities.

Johnson proclaimed the GATT Kennedy Round tariff reductions on December 16, 1967 (having concluded the negotiations by the July 1 expiration of TEA's authority to "enter into trade agreements.")[82] However, by that time, he had reluctantly conceded that he would need legislative authorization to change the ASP and anti-dumping code. In May 1968, he submitted to Congress a new Trade Expansion Act, which would implement changes to the ASP and anti-dumping laws and extend the 1962 authority through 1970. The Ways & Means Chair at the time, Wilbur Mills (D-Ark.), promptly convened a month of hearings, where witness after witness assailed the substance and constitutionality of the ASP measure. In contrast to the unauthorized Canadian auto-tariff eliminations, Congress was unwilling to accept Johnson's unauthorized trade commitments this time. Congress never had a vote on the bill, and the non-tariff aspects of the Kennedy Round never went into effect in the United States.

---

81. Quoted in Eckes, 1995, at 199.
82. Public Law 87-794 § 201(a)(1).

Regime IV. Lapse in Authority, 1967-1975

For a number of reasons, there was no delegation of trade authority between 1967 and 1975, most notably due to President Richard Nixon's focus on domestic politics during his first term. In November 1967, Sen. Eugene McCarthy (D-Minn.) declared his primary challenge against Johnson, primarily on anti-Vietnam war grounds. What began as a quixotic campaign rapidly gained adherents, and by March 1968, McCarthy had come within seven points of beating Johnson in the New Hampshire Democratic primaries. A humiliated Johnson – who had won over 60 percent of the vote only four years earlier – then announced that he would not seek the presidential nomination, which effectively ended any major policy initiatives for the rest of his term.[83]

Rapid cultural and political changes in the U.S. included a growing resentment of civil servants. This backlash emanated from both the political left and right sides of the nation. It was widely believed that liberals in the executive branch had led the United States into a foreign war they seemed unable to win. Landmark civil-rights achievements were followed by urban riots after the assassination of Martin Luther King, Jr. in April 1968. Then, Senator Bobby Kennedy was assassinated in June. These acts of violence further shook the nation and led to the political fragmentation of the August Chicago Democratic Convention, which nominated Vice President Hubert Humphrey for the top of the ticket, despite his not having participated in any primaries.[84]

In the November elections, Eisenhower's vice president Richard Nixon beat Humphrey by less than one percent of the popular vote – 43.4 to 42.7 percent. While Nixon had assiduously courted Southern Democrats in an attempt to build a new "Republican Majority," Alabama Governor George Wallace's populist third-party candidacy captured many of those voters, yielding the latter man 13.5 percent of the popular vote. Wallace's message that the Beltway had "sold out" working-class voters on both cultural and economic grounds

83. Sandbrook, 2005.
84. Solberg, 1985.

attracted significant support from union members. (The AFL-CIO estimated that a third of its members supported the Alabaman.[85]) Due to electoral-college rules, however, Nixon was able to claim 301 electoral votes to Humphrey's 199 and Wallace's 46. If Wallace had gotten a few thousand more votes in North Carolina and Tennessee, and if Humphrey had done slightly better in New Jersey and Ohio, then the election would have been thrown to the Democratic-controlled House of Representatives to decide.[86] Instead, as political scientist Thomas Schaller documented, "Nixon became the first elected president in American history to enter the White House without his party capturing either chamber of Congress."[87]

Throughout his first term, Nixon was painfully aware of his narrow election victory and his need to consolidate what he called the "Silent Majority." His response was to court Southerners and union members. He was not interested in economic matters, and saw his legacy as a partial cooptation of liberal domestic policy (through aides like Democrat Daniel Patrick Moynihan, who facilitated working relationships with the Democratic-controlled Congress), combined with executive-branch unilateralism in foreign affairs (through other aides, like Johnson administration consultant Henry Kissinger, who on the whole were wary of Congress).[88]

Despite paying lip service to "free-trade" orthodoxy, Nixon was mostly interested in politics. "What really matters in campaigns, wars, or in government is to concentrate on the big battles and win them," he told aides. "I do not want to be bothered with international monetary matters... and I will not need to see the reports on international monetary matters in the future."[89] Throughout his 1968 run and first term, he pushed textile quotas in return for the electoral support of Sen. Strom Thurmond (R-S.C.). Nixon had put Thurmond in charge of his anti-Wallace strategy.

On his first European trip as president in February 1969, Nixon told European heads of state that trade expansion was not on the agenda.

---

85. Carter, 1995, at 352.
86. Perlstein, 2008, at 354.
87. Schaller, 2006, at 40.
88. Perlstein, 2008, at 360, 370, and 395.
89. Matusow, 1998, at 126.

"I pointed out the great pressures we are under here for quotas on imports," he told advisors. "And I told them this is not the time for new breakthroughs in trade procedures. There will not be a new Kennedy Round – that's not in the cards – it's time to digest what we already have on the plate."[90]

Like it or not, international trade matters began to demand Nixon's attention, as the post-war economic order rapidly unraveled. At the 1944 Bretton Woods Conference, nations agreed to convert each other's currencies at fixed exchange rates, thereby facilitating trade and international payments. But reserve shortages in Europe after the war led countries to use the U.S. dollar instead, which the U.S. government agreed to exchange for gold at a rate of $35 an ounce. A consequence of the *de facto* dollar-gold standard was an over-accumulation of dollar reserves abroad, which now exceeded the value of gold held by the United States at Fort Knox. By 1971, European speculators were beginning to demand more gold for dollars than the U.S. Treasury possessed. Simultaneously, the United States ran its first trade deficit since 1893.[91]

In the context of looming financial instability, Nixon's economic approach became even less orthodox. He appointed former Texas governor and Democrat John Connally as Treasury secretary in February 1971. Connally said: "My basic approach is that the foreigners are out to screw us. Our job is to screw them first."[92] Nixon also appointed Pete Peterson as Assistant to the President for International Economic Affairs, but told aides beforehand that: "Trade is a two-way street... [if he's] a total free trader... he can't have the job."[93] Neither Connally nor Peterson disappointed. Peterson maintained that: "our [trade] partners no longer need special crutches. In fact, as is sometimes the case, patients may be inclined to throw them at the doctor."[94] Connally advocated for U.S. adoption of Japanese-style industrial policy. Within months, Nixon was conveying their message,

---

90. Matusow, 1998, at 119.
91. Matusow, 1998, at 123-126 and 144-148.
92. Matusow, 1998, at 117.
93. Matusow, 1998, at 132.
94. Matusow, 1998, at 134.

telling Peterson in June 1971 that while previous administrations had used trade for foreign policy purposes, we "must use it as [an] instrument of our domestic policy, e.g. jobs."[95]

Nixon instructed his team to, in historian Rick Perlstein's words, "win the election by doing whatever he had to do to make the economy *appear* to boom in the run-up to the 1972 elections, no matter the longer-term consequences of the techniques it took to do it."[96] Indeed, in August 1971, Nixon showed a willingness to upend completely the post-war economic order if it helped him win an election. After a presidential retreat at Camp David, Nixon proclaimed through executive order that he was abandoning the dollar-gold standard, and imposed an across-the-board import surcharge – an additional tariff on all imported goods – of 10 percent, along with other wage and price controls.[97] In the absence of delegated trade authority from Congress, Nixon invoked the Trading with the Enemy Act of 1917 as the legal basis for declaring the new tariffs, arguing that international financial instability constituted the sort of "national emergency" under which the 1917 act granted the executive broad authority to restrict imports.[98]

The surcharge was designed to reduce imports by making them more expensive, and thereby to balance trade. In December 1971, Nixon phased out the relatively small surcharge, which only had a modest impact on trade flows. (Indeed, its most notable effect was to force other countries to the negotiating table, which led to the Smithsonian Agreement on exchange rates. Under this agreement, European countries as well as Japan and Canada agreed to appreciate their currencies relative to the dollar in a move towards floating currency exchange rates.)

However, the underlying political goal had been accomplished: Nixon had established his populist credentials. Polls showed that 75 percent of the public approved of his August 1971 "New Economic Policy."[99]

---

95. Matusow, 1998, at 137.
96. Perlstein, 2008, at 599.
97. Dale, 1971; Silk, 1971. Only certain commodities like oil were exempted.
98. Irwin, 2012, at 37.
99. Perlstein, 2008, at 603.

In the 1972 election, he won by almost exactly Johnson's 1964 margin – 60.7 percent of the popular vote. This translated to a whopping 520 out of 537 electoral votes. Despite Nixon's strong showing at the presidential level, however, Democrats still maintained their majorities in both chambers. This fact was extremely frustrating to his administration, which had to turn its attention on how to work with – or at least divide and confuse – the Democratic-labor coalition.

Regime V. Executive Branch Hegemony over Non-Tariff Rules: Fast Track's Rise and Fall Through 2012

a. Boarding Nixon's Fast Track, 1973-1975

While Nixon's first term included "more new regulation… than in any other presidency since the New Deal" (in historian Allen Matusow's words), he "entered the second term determined to reverse this trend."[100] George Shultz had replaced Connally as Treasury secretary in June 1972, and convinced Nixon that trade was going to be the predominant tool for exercising U.S. influence in the world. He maintained that other countries' non-tariff barriers were a primary constraint on U.S. exports, and thus an obstacle to sustained U.S. trade balance.[101]

Labor politics were also in flux. While the AFL-CIO supported the Kennedy Round and TEA, trade-related job losses among its members were leading the federation to formulate specific proposals aimed at ensuring that trade expansion continued to benefit American workers. In 1971, the AFL-CIO drafted legislation co-sponsored by Rep. James Burke (D-Mass.) and Sen. Vance Hartke (D-Ind.). The bill would have frozen imports at 1960s levels using quotas, limited the export of U.S.-developed technology, and increased the taxes that U.S. multinationals paid on their overseas operations.[102]

As author John Judis put it, the Burke-Hartke bill "opened debate over an entirely new area of public and democratic control of corporate behavior. It was based on the premise that the public had a right to regulate what an American corporation did internationally when American jobs were at stake… more than any single debate, it expressed the basic conflict that the post-Bretton Woods world economy was creating between business on the one hand and labor and movements" on the other. And big business fought ferociously to make sure it never became law.[103]

---

100. Matusow, 1998, at 241.
101. Beckman, 1972; Gannon, 1973.
102. H.R. 10914 in the 92nd Congress, and H.R. 62 in the 93rd Congress. Also called the Foreign Trade and Investment Act.
103. Judis, 2001, at 114-115.

Nixon, who benefited from the AFL-CIO's unusual lack of endorsement for the Democratic candidate in the recent presidential campaign, began his second term still courting labor. In February 1973, he attended the annual AFL-CIO convention in Key Biscayne, Florida. Nixon expressed his sympathy for workers displaced by imports, but did not endorse Burke-Hartke. He let slip that he had another proposal in mind that would allow more flexibility while achieving many of the same results. Labor staffers suggested that they had won the president over to their approach.[104] Echoing Shultz, the AFL-CIO's Nathaniel Goldfinger wrote in the *New York Times* that non-tariff barriers abroad were creating barriers to U.S. trade balance. Among the causes of American decline were:

> "The spread of managed national economies. Governments now have direct and indirect barriers to imports, as well as various types of subsidies for exports. The result is that imports surge into the huge American market, the most open market to imports of all major industrial countries, while the expansion of United States exports is retarded or blocked by the practices of foreign governments."[105]

In April 1973, Nixon unveiled his legislative proposal, which he pitched as a comprehensive package to restore America's trade balance.[106] *The Washington Post* editorial board summarized the situation the president found himself in: "Mr. Nixon has usually been able to arrange his affairs in a fashion that leaves Congress pretty well out of our international relations. Now, before he can negotiate with the rest of the world on the crucial issues of trade, he must have a kind of authority that only Congress can give him."[107]

The Trade Reform Act of 1973, H.R. 6767, introduced by Wilbur Mills on April 10, 1973, included a new delegation of tariff-proclamation authority. Section 401 of the act featured authority for the president to apply new import surcharges, and set their rate. The surcharges

---

104. Shabecoff, 1973.
105. Goldfinger, 1973.
106. Beckman, 1972; Shabecoff, 1973.
107 WP, 1973.

could be applied on a country-by-country or across-the-board basis. It allowed for certain exclusions, such as for oil. The Ways & Means Committee's report on the bill went so far as to advocate that import surcharges should be the *preferred* means for countries to deal with balance-of-payments problems.[108]

Yet the most dramatic feature of the legislation was its new expansion of executive authority over *non-tariff* issues. Nixon's team saw foreign governments' procurement practices as a growing obstacle to U.S. exports and thus an impediment to closing the trade deficit. Thus, they wanted authority to enter into trade agreements that would include disciplines on government procurement and other related matters – *trade agreement disciplines that implicitly would also apply to U.S. non-tariff domestic policies.* They strongly implied that the trade deficit could be resolved by reducing foreign "non-tariff barriers." Said one administration official:

> "With the success of the Kennedy Round in 1967 in reducing tariffs among the world's major trading nations, non-tariff practices have become the major impediment to fair competition and the free flow of goods in international trade. Major attention will be given in the Multilateral Trade Negotiations to eliminating and reducing these trade-distorting measures. The job will not be easy as many of these practices are imbedded [sic] in national laws and policies."[109]

In making his case for non-tariff powers, Nixon invoked Congress' rejection of the elements of the Kennedy Round implementing legislation that enacted non-tariff provisions of the agreement. Although the executive branch had caused this outcome by signing an agreement that extended beyond the authority Congress had granted it, Nixon argued that Congress had embarrassed the nation, and that countries would refuse to negotiate with the United States in the future. In reality, the new GATT Tokyo Round of negotiation was launched in September 1973, a year before Congress had agreed

---

108. WM, 1973b, at 27-33.
109. SF, 1974, at 173.

to new presidential trade authority. Shultz claimed: "the fact that our trade bill is still under congressional review does not impede our ability to participate actively and fully [in GATT talks] at this stage."[110]

The 1973 act represented a wholesale re-envisioning of Congress' fundamental constitutional responsibilities. While the tariff-proclamation authority was a continuation of past practice, Fast Track delegated to the president for the first time the authority to enter into an agreement that included non-tariff matters and to do so before Congress voted on the agreement's terms. In fact, Nixon's original Fast Track proposal would have allowed the president to negotiate and sign trade agreements covering tariff and non-tariff matters, and to proclaim tariff levels *and changes to U.S. non-tariff laws* unilaterally for a period of five years.

Congress would be given 90 days notice before the president entered into any trade agreement that made changes to non-tariff legislation. However, the president would not have to explain in any detail what U.S. laws he contemplated changing. *After* proclaiming any tariff or law changes, the president was to transmit copies of any such proclamations to Congress. No congressional vote was required, and the proclamations automatically took effect if neither chamber "vetoed" the proposal via a disapproval resolution within 90 days.

In a letter to Mills on June 13, 1973, Nixon's Justice Department argued that the authorities to enter into non-tariff trade agreements and to impose import surcharges were constitutional, and cited Supreme Court rulings from *Hampton* to *Field*.[111]

---

110. Halloran, 1973.
111. WM, 1973a, at 326-330. In a 1967 article, legal scholar John Jackson maintained that these rulings, coupled with the fact that RTAA hearings had discussed GATT issues, indicate: "The practice of all three branches of our government recognizes the legal existence of GATT." In the same article, he quotes 1955 testimony by John Foster Dulles (Eisenhower's secretary of state) that, "I don't believe that this law which has remained on the books 21 years unchallenged is constitutional." Nonetheless, Jackson's article quoted the aforementioned angry questioning of a Truman administration official by Republican Sen. Eugene Millikin in 1949, showing that the matter was far from settled, as Jackson himself discovered in 1973, when he faced tough congressional questions on the scope of GATT non-tariff issues. Legal scholar Lawrence Tribe criticized the Jackson-Dulles analysis. In *Field v. Clark*, Tribe writes, "the Supreme Court upheld a proclamation statute – an act of Congress authorizing the president to take particular action upon finding certain conditions to be met – by relying in part on the value as precedent of legislative practice... The Court's decision nearly a century later in Chadha [when the legislative veto was overturned], however, makes plain that an historical pedigree extending back only a matter of decades is insufficient to sustain the constitutionality of even a frequent congressional practice that conflicts with constitutional text and structure." See Tribe, 1995, at 1281.

Shotgunning the Balance of Powers

> John Connally summed up the Nixon administration's approach to executive-legislative relations with this pithy assertion: "If the legislature wants to give you a new power – you take it. Put it in the corner like an old shotgun. You never know when you might need it."[112]

> One congressperson returned to this frame decades later, noting that "Fast Track operates like a gun to our head – no amendments, no reservations."[113]

In addition to the tariff and non-tariff provisions, the package included more trade adjustment assistance. And to counter concerns that limiting Congress' role would hinder private-sector input into U.S. trade-agreement formulation, the proposal established a system of formal trade-advisory committees that would be comprised of private-sector representatives.

Nixon had kicked off 1973 trying to get labor's backing for his delegation proposal. After the initial collaborative gestures, however, both he and Mills sidelined labor. As early as April, labor leaders recognized the Nixon-Mills bill did not meet their minimum standards, and AFL-CIO President Meany promised to push mandatory Burke-Hartke style quotas as an amendment. But the Ways & Means Committee voted down the Meany amendment in July.[114] A reporter for the *Washington Post* summed up the situation, noting that, "the landmark legislative proposal gives organized labor none of its maximum demands."[115] Meany declared that the Nixon-Mills bill was "worse than no legislation at all."[116]

The bid for greater presidential authority and an expanded scope for trade agreements did not go unnoticed in Congress. In the month-long Ways & Means Committee hearings, the very first comment fired at administration officials came from Rep. Al Ullman (D-Ore.), who

---

112. Perlstein, 2008, at 600.
113. Sen. Ernest Hollings (D-S.C.), quoted in Cloud, 1991.
114. McKinsey, 1973; and Dale, 1973b.
115. Berger, 1973.
116. LAT, 1973.

said: "My problem with your proposal, and I think this perhaps will be your major obstacle in getting this legislation through, is the degree to which we are delegating broad new powers to the executive."[117]

At another point in the hearings, Mills, newly concerned with the domestic implications of his own bill, raised the specter of non-trade laws being challenged as barriers to trade in new trade agreements, echoing the concerns that GOP Senator Eugene Millikin raised decades before in the GATT hearings. Nixon administration official John Jackson batted this criticism away, saying: "There are some other possibilities in the area of how a government will allow another government or another society's firms to set up offices in the country, in our country, for instance, or to provide certain kinds of facilities. Now, sometimes these are termed, I grant you they are out on the fringe, but sometimes they are termed nontariff barriers." Mills retorted: "Do any of our health laws enter into this, sanitation laws?" Jackson replied: "Yes. I am sure that there are such, there are aspects of those laws that could be termed nontariff barriers."[118] While the administration downplayed the implications of Fast Track for non-trade policy, a review of the extensive hearings reveals testimony from a Japanese business advocate that listed "Buy Local" and "Buy America" provisions in almost every state as something to be eliminated in the GATT negotiations.[119]

Mills was prescient. The record would show Fast Track to be a powerful mechanism for skirting Congress' control of domestic non-trade policy, and forcing changes to the very policy areas the chairman had identified. (For instance, implementation of the Fast Tracked GATT Uruguay Round in 1995 included changes to U.S. meat-safety and inspection regulations. This weakened the previously standing policy that allowed only imports of meat and poultry meeting U.S. standards.[120]) At the time, however, Mills and his committee were

---

117. WM, 1973a, at 183.
118. WM, 1973a, at 447-448.
119. WM, 1973a, at 1060.
120. See e.g. 60 Fed. Reg. 38667, July 28, 1995 which explains why the WTO's Sanitary and Phytosanitary Agreement and the Uruguay Round Implementing Act require a change to USDA rules. The regulation removes the requirement that meat and poultry may only be imported from countries with safety standards equal to U.S. law to the WTO-required standard of accepting imports that meet 'equivalent' foreign standards, noting that doing otherwise could be deemed an illegal non-tariff barrier.

reassured that their concerns were misplaced. For instance, Ways & Means documents reveal that the committee assumed that the kinds of non-tariff negotiations being contemplated would lend themselves to simple conversions to tariff equivalents. They believed that this would involve, to make a purely hypothetical example, converting a 500-shipment-a-year cheese quota to a 25 percent cheese tariff. Perhaps they simply could not fully envision future questions, such as: what is the tariff equivalent of the Buy American government procurement preference or some U.S. states' limits on foreign ownership of farm land? These are just two aspects of policy which were targeted for curtailment in subsequent Fast Tracked trade negotiations.

The Ways & Means Committee report on the bill revealed further insights into the committee's expectations on process. "The committee has been assured, however, that due to the complexities involved and, in particular, to the unique legislative character [of non-tariff barriers], … that the adoption of [changes to non-tariff laws] will be the subject of a request for affirmative congressional approval through the normal legislative process."[121] In other words, Mills trusted President Nixon to refrain voluntarily from using the vast new authorities which had been granted to him by the committee.

It is intriguing to consider the role of the Ways & Means Committee in agreeing to such a major delegation of congressional authority. The revenue committee had jurisdiction over trade because tariffs had been a primary source of government revenue in the republic's early years. But by 1973, tariffs constituted only 1 percent of government revenue.[122] And in any case, since 1890, Congress had regularly delegated authority over tariffs to the executive branch, which had built up agencies like the Tariff Commission (now USITC) to make recommendations on the issue.

However, the scope of non-tariff pacts contemplated under Fast Track would deeply delve into numerous *other* congressional committees'

---

121. WM, 1973b, at 25.

122. Total 1974 government receipts taken from U.S. Census Bureau, *Statistical Abstract of the United States, 1974,* at 221. Total 1974 duties collected taken from U.S. Census Bureau, *Statistical Abstract of the United States, 1984,* at 841.

jurisdiction, including many delicate domestic-policy issues not appropriate for executive-branch control, such as immigration, patent and copyright terms, food safety, banking regulation, public health measures, environmental protection and government procurement. The historical record hints at some congressional awareness of the implications of this expansion of jurisdiction. Nonetheless, to this day, many in Congress are surprised to learn that the WTO or NAFTA include binding rules regarding non-trade issues covered by the jurisdiction of committees outside Ways & Means and Finance. Regardless, decades of jurisdictional inertia meant that at this critical juncture these committees, whose original remit was tariff revenue, were empowered to facilitate the executive branch's stunning grab of wide new swaths of Congress' non-trade and trade authority. It is perhaps not surprising that most of the House committee chairs voted against the 1973 Fast Track.[123]

The Ways & Means leaders from both parties – Acting Chair Ullman[124] and Ranking Member Herman Schneebeli (R-Pa.) – rounded up support for Fast Track, and controlled a combined six hours of debate when it came to the House floor on December 10, 1973. Even though a majority of Democrats opposed the measure, the bill's opponents only got one hour of floor-time to present their views. James Burke (of the Burke-Hartke bill) made the most of the scarce time, giving a blistering speech:

> "There is no question that this bill would make the President of the United States the foreign trade czar of this Nation. While it is conceivable that there would be times

123. The jurisdiction of at least nine House committees other than Ways & Means could be reasonably construed to be impacted by the international commercial agreements, such as WTO and NAFTA, enabled by Fast Track. These committees are contemplated for consultations under provisions of the Trade Reform, Accountability, Development and Employment (TRADE) Act introduced on June 4, 2008, which outlines a new mechanism for trade agreement negotiations and approval. A majority of the then-chairs of the affected committees voted against Fast Track in 1973. The six opposed include: William Poage (D-Texas) of Agriculture; Carl Perkins (D-Ky.) of Education & Labor; Harley Staggers (D-W.V.) of Energy & Commerce; Wright Patman (D-Texas) of Banking & Currency (now Financial Services); Thomas Morgan (D-Pa.) of Foreign Affairs; and Peter Rodino (D-N.J.) of Judiciary. Only James Haley (D-Fla.) of Natural Resources and John Blatnik (D-Minn.) of Transportation supported the legislation. Mills was absent, but acting Ways & Means chair Al Ullman also voted aye. Small Business, the final committee contemplated for consultations under the 2008 TRADE Act, did not yet exist in 1973.
124. Mills was sick during the floor proceedings.

when I might agree with his actions, it is also certain that there would be many times when I would disagree. But, agree or disagree, there would be little Congress could do, having voted in this bill to give the President a free hand to conduct this nation's foreign trade as he determines best over the next 5 years... taken all together, this massive delegation of authority to the President constitutes a virtual abdication of congressional authority and interest in the foreign trade area.

"In my opinion, the Founding Fathers clearly and carefully assessed the importance of the power to levy duties and in other ways to regulate foreign commerce... If regulation of foreign trade was of crucial importance to our Founding Fathers... of how much more greater concern should the conduct of foreign trade be to a Congress today? Not only is foreign trade inextricably wound up with the conduct of this nation's foreign policy but it is crucial to the Nation's whole domestic economic policy, both monetary and fiscal, as well as its full employment policy...

"To mention the Gulf of Tonkin is to mention the most flagrant example of congressional abdication of authority, in this instance, Congress' exclusive power to declare war. Anyone who has been in this body the last 10 years knows firsthand the tremendous effort it took to gradually regain some semblance of congressional authority in this area, culminating as it did only with the decision to end the bombing of Cambodia on August 15 of this year.

"How this same Congress a few weeks later can even contemplate abdicating authority in the foreign trade area is beyond my comprehension. To allow the President – and in effect faceless bureaucrats downtown, answerable to no one – authority to make the vital decisions over the next 5 years in foreign trade is for Congress to bow out of one of the most important areas of decision-making in the government today. History – and not ancient, but very recent history – if it has taught this Congress anything, it is that power lost today in the name of greater ease of decision-making and flexibility for negotiators, is power hard to regain tomorrow in the name of constitutional prerogatives...

"Now we all know that life today is more complicated than it was in the days of our Founding Fathers. Certainly relations with foreign governments are no exception. Doubtlessly matters requiring, as trade policies do today, detailed negotiations with foreign governments necessitate the day-to-day participation of executive department personnel. Furthermore, it has never been anything but difficult since the beginning of time for governments to resolve conflicting demands between the dual needs of determining national foreign policy objectives and providing negotiators with sufficient flexibility to negotiate the best possible arrangements with foreign governments. Granted these conflicting demands make it extremely difficult to legislate in the foreign trade area. However, I do not think we acquit ourselves with any great distinction when we avoid drafting necessarily difficult and complicated legislation and simply give the executive department authority to make the tough decisions in this area. In my opinion, these decisions are important enough to be either made directly or clearly charted by the legislative branch of the government. But instead of wrestling with the problem of providing sufficiently clear guidelines for our negotiators in the very important international conferences scheduled for the near future, we have left it for the President to do... Instead of being called the Trade Reform Act of 1973, it should be labeled the Trade Power Transfer Act."[125]

---

125. Rep. James Burke (D-Mass.), *Congressional Record*, Dec. 10, 1973, at H40533-H40534.

On December 11, 1973, the bill passed the House on a 272-140 vote, offering Nixon unprecedented powers even as congressional investigations of the Watergate break-in intensified.[126]

Surely the Senate, that traditional bastion of legislative-branch prerogative, would block the overreaching Fast Track proposal. In fact, it did, amending the legislation to require Congress to have a vote to approve or disapprove trade deals negotiated by the executive branch under the delegated authority. In negotiations held during the summer of 1974, Sen. Herman Talmadge (D-Ga.) succeeded in forcing the executive branch to admit that there were only a few non-negotiable aspects of the bill.

Those aspects were: that congressional consideration of trade agreements should be time limited, and that they should be given an up or down vote once they were negotiated (so as to avoid the Kennedy Round situation where Congress simply refused to vote on non-tariff implementing legislation). The administration claimed that a guaranteed vote would reassure negotiating partners that once negotiations were complete, Congress would be forced to accept or reject the outcome.[127] (This later proved to be untrue, when changes were made in 2009 to FTAs signed by the Bush administration under Fast Track in 2007.)

The final bill ordered the president to take rapid action in order to have the GATT adopt "international fair labor standards" including public petition and dispute settlement.[128] And, when one final concession was made – this time related to a provision for the trade treatment of Soviet bloc countries that limited Jewish emigration[129] – an amended

126. Trade Reform Act of 1973, H.R. 10710, was approved on a 272-140 vote on Dec. 11, 1973. 121 Democrats opposed, and only 112 supported. Republicans voted 160-19 in favor of the bill.
127. Marks and Malmgren, 1975, at 339.
128. Public Law 93-618 § 121(a)(4). However, because the structure of Fast Track allowed executive branch negotiators unilaterally to decide whether it had met Congress' negotiating objectives and to sign and seal an agreement's text before Congress voted on it, labor rights provisions were not included in the GATT deal negotiated under this Fast Track. Labor rights provisions were also not included in NAFTA or the GATT Uruguay Round that were negotiated under the 1988 grant of Fast Track, which also included fairly robust labor rights objectives. However, the most robust labor rights provisions included in any U.S. trade agreements were included in four FTAs negotiated by President George W. Bush under a Fast Track delegation that included negotiating objectives strictly limiting labor rights terms.
129. 19 U.S.C. § 2432.

Fast Track was approved by the Senate and then a final conferenced version was passed in the Senate on a 72-4 vote on the last day of a lame duck session on December 20, 1974, months after Nixon had resigned.[130]

The conferenced bill was not even printed for the House vote, which was literally the last vote of the lame duck session, also occurring on December 20. At this moment of minimum political accountability, 75 House members and 23 Senate members abstained from voting, including Chairman Mills and Sen. Talmadge, two of the congresspeople most responsible for getting Fast Track moving in Congress. The bill was signed into law by President Gerald Ford in January of the following year.

Core Aspects of Fast Track Trade Authority Delegation

- Allowed the executive branch to select countries for, set the substance of, negotiate and then sign trade agreements – all before Congress had a vote on the matter.

- Required the executive branch to notify Congress 90 calendar days before signing and entering into an agreement.[131]

- Empowered the executive branch to write lengthy implementing legislation for each pact on its own, without committee mark ups. Because the process circumvented normal congressional processes, congressional committees could not amend these executive-authored bills even though they would alter wide swaths of U.S. non-trade, domestic law and policy, forcing it to be altered so as to conform to each agreement's requirements, and would formally adopt the agreement texts as U.S. law. As a concession to congressional decorum, the executive branch agreed to participate in "non" or "mock" hearings and markups of the legislation by the trade committees.

---

130. On Dec. 13, the Senate passed a pre-conference version of Fast Track (H.R. 10710) on a 77-4 vote (Democrats: 45-3; Republicans: 32-1). On Dec. 20, the Senate passed the final bill on a 72-4 vote (Democrats: 41-3; Republicans 31-1). But when the House voted on the conference version, a printed copy had not even been furnished to members, who were forced to rely on Ullman's word that the Senate had improved the bill. On Dec. 20, the House passed the final bill on a 333-26 margin (Democrats: 176-25; Republicans: 147-11). As Rep. Charles Dent (D-Pa.) pointed out in the House floor debate on final passage. "This is one bill that no one wants to hear anything about, because they might hear something that is in opposition to their views. The trade bill is just like someone who starts taking dope. People who take dope know it is wrong, they know it is unhealthy, they know that in the end it will kill them, but they keep on taking it."
131. Public Law 93-618 § 102(e)(1).

However, this is a practice, not a requirement. In 2008, President Bush chose to ignore this practice and exercise the president's Fast Track right to force a vote on an agreement, submitting the U.S.-Colombia FTA to Congress without an informal agreement with congressional leaders on timing or mock mark ups, defying congressional leaders' objections to the pact's submission at that time.[132]

- Once the executive branch submitted such a bill, the agreement itself and various supporting materials to Congress, the House and Senate were required to vote on the implementing legislation and the attached agreement within 90 legislative days.

- Such bills were automatically referred to the House Ways & Means and Senate Finance Committees. (In the 2002 Fast Track bill, the House and Senate Agriculture committees also got a formal referral). However, if a committee failed to report out the bill within 45 legislative days from when the president submitted the legislation to Congress, the bill was automatically discharged to the floor for a vote.

- A House floor vote was required no later than 15 legislative days after the bill was reported or discharged from committee. Thus, within 60 legislative days, the House was required to vote on whatever agreement the president had signed, and whatever legislation changing U.S. laws he had written to implement the package.

- The Finance Committee was allowed an additional 15 days after the House vote, at which time the bill was automatically discharged to the Senate floor for a vote required within 15 legislative days.

- The floor votes in both the House and Senate were highly privileged. Normal congressional floor procedures were waived, including Senate unanimous consent and debate and cloture rules, and no amendments were allowed. Debate was limited to 20 hours – even in the Senate.

- Once the president provided Congress with notice of his intent to sign an agreement, he was authorized to sign after 90 calendar days. However,

---

132. The House responded to Bush's exercise of this aspect of Fast Track by reasserting Congress' constitutional prerogatives and removing the 60-day mandatory vote requirement from the agreement. This was possible because, as a technical matter, the pre-set floor-vote procedures aspect of Fast Track is a "rule" of the House and Senate, which the chambers can change by majority vote. (This was a necessary compromise for the Fast Track floor-consideration rules to be constitutional.) However, such a rule change has only occurred in this one instance in the history of Fast Track. The various trade-authority delegations have also contained procedures for Congress to take an agreement off the Fast Track through the passage of disapproval resolutions. For various reasons described below, these procedures have been largely ineffectual. For more information on disapproval resolutions, see Forbes, 2008.

there was no mandatory timeline for him to submit formal implementing legislation and start the 90-legislative day vote clock. Thus, an agreement's legal text finalized just minutes before the delegation authority expired could be sent to Congress even years later with Fast Track's procedural restrictions still in effect.

- Once a president submitted an agreement under Fast Track, that agreement's Fast Track extraordinary treatment was considered to be "used up" – or so thought the few lawyers and policymakers who pondered the matter. They assumed that if Congress adjourned before the mandatory vote clock ran out or if Congress voted against the agreement, Fast Track for that agreement expired. Thus, if it were to be submitted again for a later vote, normal congressional floor procedures would apply.[133] However, when George W. Bush submitted the Colombia FTA over congressional leaders' objections and then House leaders obtained a majority for a rule change to stop the mandatory vote clock, the House and Senate parliamentarians split on their analysis of what it meant that the 111th Congress concluded without a vote on the pact. The House parliamentarian deemed the Fast Track rules to no longer apply when the Colombia FTA was resubmitted for a vote in the next Congress, but the Senate parliamentarian ruled that the special procedures did apply and normal Senate rules were suspended.

- An advisory-committee system was established to obtain private sector input on trade-agreement negotiations from presidentially appointed advisors.[134] This system, which remains in effect, is organized by sector and industry and includes over 600 advisors comprised mainly of industry representatives. Throughout trade talks, these individuals obtain special access to confidential negotiating documents to which the public has no access. (While members of Congress and congressional staff with security clearance had formerly been provided access to these documents and also to drafts of actual trade agreement texts, with respect to negotiations for the Trans-Pacific Partnership (TPP) FTA, access by Congress to draft agreement text has been denied and security-cleared staff have been denied access even to U.S. proposals to the TPP negotiations.) The advisory committees are required to file reports on proposed trade agreements. The Fast Track legislation called

---

133. For details on House Parliamentarian's ruling on the matter, see IUT, 2006b.
134. Public Law 93-618 § 135.

for establishment of private sector advisory committees for numerous sectors, but not consumer, faith, health, or environmental interests.[135]

- The 1974 Fast Track also elevated the Special Trade Representative (STR) to the cabinet level, and required the Executive Office of the Presidency to house the agency. While other cabinet-level positions tend to be responsive to a pre-defined constituency (Agriculture and farmers, for instance), the STR was unique in that its only real constituency was the president, the gatekeeper committees of Congress, and the hundreds of industry advisors on the trade advisory committees. And its main goal was proliferation of trade negotiations. The 1979 Fast Track changed the name of the STR to the U.S. Trade Representative (USTR).

- The 2002 Fast Track created an additional requirement for 90-day notice to the gatekeeper committees *before* negotiations could begin, but neither the gatekeepers nor the executive were required to take any further action after receiving this notice.[136]

The context of the 93rd Congress (1973-74) provides some clues as to how such a revolutionary delegation of congressional authority might have passed. The United States was experiencing high unemployment and running trade deficits for the first time in a century, and the executive branch was promising Fast Tracked implementation of trade measures like import surcharges to restore balance. Some trade advocates fretted that, "the Administration trade bill, which would have been regarded as drastically protectionist a decade ago, now represents the liberal wing of the congressional debate."[137] Also, Nixon officials premised their campaign on a view of the global economy that seems quaint in retrospect, telling Ways & Means that: "China is largely an agricultural country… we don't know for sure how much trade they are prepared to have."[138]

---

135. Public Citizen, 1991. Labor was mentioned in the statute and a labor advisory committee was established. In the 1984 Fast Track (Public Law 98-573 § 306(c)(2)(A)), a new advisory committee was added for representatives of state and local governments and their associations. Lawsuits in the 1990s resulted in establishment of a Trade and Environment advisory committee, but it was comprised of equal numbers of industry- and environmental-group representatives, deadlocking its reports and eventually causing some of the environmental representatives to resign. See MH, 2003.
136. Public Law 107-210 § 2104(a).
137. Quote of C. Fred Bergsten, in Jones, 1973.
138. WM, 1973a, at 212 and 263.

Perhaps most critically, U.S. trade agreements to date had concerned only traditional trade matters – cutting tariffs and lifting quotas. Thus, the final Senate deal may have seemed like a tolerable protection of congressional authority, given Congress' notion of what would be included in trade agreements. After all, Congress had delegated tariff-proclamation authority before. Legislators did not foresee expansive pacts like the WTO and NAFTA, which would require changes to a wide variety of non-trade policies either through implementing legislation or later to comply with dispute resolution rulings from foreign enforcement tribunals established by the pacts. Additionally, Congress was reassured that the scope of future non-tariff provisions would still be limited – mostly to issues like quotas or customs valuation methods.

The debate on the initial establishment of Fast Track also revealed the split between the "gatekeeper" committees – Ways & Means and Finance – and the rest of Congress. The deal-making Mills encapsulated the approach that some Democratic and Republican gatekeeper chairs would take over the years. He said of Nixon: "He is asking for more of a grant of authority than we have given any other President. This is a touchy subject in Congress right now. But … I'm for it."[139] In 1973-74, Rep. Richard Bolling (D-Mo.) tried to address the considerable concentration of jurisdiction and power in these committees by attempting to remove trade from Ways & Means' jurisdiction. The effort, led from Bolling's Select Committee on Committees, would have given trade jurisdiction to the Foreign Affairs Committee. Mills organized vigorously against the effort, making common cause with labor groups that opposed Bolling's accompanying proposal to remove education from the House Education & Labor Committee's jurisdiction. In September 1974, the House Rules Committee reported out Bolling's plan, but in the form of a Democratic Caucus-backed substitute that did not include the jurisdictional changes. The House passed that bill by a wide margin.[140]

---

139. Dale, 1973b. For scandals affecting various Ways & Means chairs, see Remini, 2006, at 442-443, 455, and 480-481.
140. Zelizer, 2004, at 143-151.

In sum, Fast Track was passed because of a unique set of historical circumstances. Only in the midst of a global economic breakdown whose roots were poorly understood would Fast Track's shift of power away from Congress to the executive branch via highly unorthodox provisions on non-tariff issues have been considered a possible economic remedy. Opposition from the Republican Party – for 30 years the voice of constitutional criticism of the Reciprocal Trade Agreements Act – was absent: *their president* was in charge this time. Thus, the Nixon White House's disregard for separation of powers, which likely played a major role in the conception of Fast Track, was tolerated. Democratic criticism was split. On one side was a labor camp that bet everything on a strategy of mandatory quotas, thought it had an ally in Nixon, and lost big. On the other side was a foreign-policy camp led by Sen. Henry "Scoop" Jackson (D-Wash.) and Rep. Charles Vanik (D-Ohio), who didn't debate the bill's constitutional or trade implications but focused on the bill as a vehicle to pressure Jewish emigration from the Soviet Union. Other Democratic leaders just wanted to make a deal, and had perhaps not thought critically about the proposal. Mills' once sharp mind in particular had been weakened by addiction to alcohol since 1969 and painkillers since 1972, according to biographer Julian Zelizer.[141] So when legal scholars like Hal Shapiro say that Fast Track "is not necessary,"[142] it must be added that it was also not inevitable.

Yet, as the decades passed, fewer and fewer members of Congress remained in office who understood Fast Track as an *extraordinary* forfeiture of Congress' constitutional trade authority in favor of executive branch control. Even fewer were those who had operated in the pre-Fast Track context, when Congress had a more robust role. Thus, for a generation, Fast Track became the presumptive mechanism for trade-agreement negotiation and approval.

---

141. Zelizer, 1998, at 334-336, and 350-353.
142. Shapiro, 2006, at 161.

Wilbur Mills (D-Ark.) Chair of the House Ways & Means Committee at the time Fast Track was first established (pictured left), with then-Rep. George H.W. Bush (R-Texas) (pictured center), at a 1966 reception for freshmen members of Congress. From 1989-1993, Bush used Fast Track as president to negotiate NAFTA and the WTO. In 1973-74, Mills played an instrumental role in getting the original Fast Track through Congress. However, in late 1974, Mills stepped down from his chairmanship of the Ways and Means Committee after several public incidents related to his struggles with alcoholism.[143] Also pictured is Rep. John Byrnes (R-Wis.).

---

143. Mills was involved in a late night traffic incident in Washington in October1974. Mills was intoxicated, and his face was injured from a scuffle with Annabelle Battistella, better known as Fanne Foxe, a stripper from Argentina. When police approached the car, Foxe leapt from the car and jumped into the nearby Tidal Basin in an attempt to escape. Despite the scandal, Mills was re-elected to Congress in November 1974. However on November 30, 1974, Mills, seemingly drunk, was accompanied by Foxe's husband onstage at The Pilgrim Theatre in Boston, a burlesque house where Foxe was performing. He held a press conference from Foxe's dressing room. Soon after this second public incident, Mills stepped down from his chairmanship of the Ways & Means Committee, acknowledged his alcoholism, joined Alcoholics Anonymous, and checked himself into a treatment center.

b. Fast Track's First Use Expands Scope of GATT to Non-Tariffs Issues, 1975-1980

The Tokyo Round of GATT negotiations started in 1973, and by 1979, the Jimmy Carter administration brought the completed deal back to Congress for an expedited up-or-down, Fast Tracked vote. The first use of Fast Track revealed a problem that has only been exacerbated with time. Fast Track did not provide Congress any mechanism to review agreement texts to ensure they met Congress' negotiating objectives (which, in the 1974 act were listed in the form of "steps to be taken toward GATT revision" in Section 121). There was also no process by which the executive branch – if it ignored congressional negotiating objectives and instructions – would lose Fast Track's rights to sign an agreement before a congressional vote. Thus, Fast Track gave the executive extraordinary power to determine unilaterally the contents of a given trade agreement.

Thus, the final Tokyo Round agreement included a series of unprecedented provisions on various non-tariff matters that extended far beyond the quotas and customs valuation issues discussed with the trade committees during the 1973-74 Fast Track debate – let alone the original mid-century hearings on the GATT. Yet the notion of expanding into non-tariff issues was so controversial with the other 102 GATT signatory countries that the only way to even broach these subjects was for the resulting outcomes not to become full GATT agreements. Rather, the new expanded non-tariff rules were only signed by some participants. These plurilateral agreements became known as the Tokyo Round "codes," and were signed by only a relatively small number of (mainly industrialized) GATT members, including the United States.[144]

---

144. The new non-tariff issues were dealt with in "plurilateral" agreements, meaning they were not binding except on countries that specifically opted into them. (This was called the "GATT a la carte" approach, as opposed to the Uruguay Round's "single package" approach.) The Tokyo Round codes included the Agreement on Government Procurement; the Agreement on Import Licensing Procedures; and the Agreement on Technical Barriers to Trade (sometimes called the Standards Code). There were also codes interpreting exiting GATT rules, such as on subsidies and countervailing measures (interpreting Articles 6, 16 and 23 of the GATT); customs valuation (interpreting Article 7); anti-dumping (interpreting Article 6, replacing the Kennedy Round code). Lastly, there were three sector-specific codes (the Bovine Meat Arrangement, International Dairy Arrangement and Trade in Civil Aircraft). See Public Law 96-39 § 2(c); Jackson, 1997, at 166.

The texts of these non-tariff agreements delved deeply into matters previously in the exclusive jurisdiction of domestic legislatures, including the most domestic of all matters: how domestic tax dollars should be spent in procuring goods and services. The Tokyo Round procurement agreement not only required that U.S. government procurement officials treat foreign and domestic goods and producers equally – a direct conflict with expansive Buy American laws then in effect – but set forth limits on what technical specifications Congress could establish for desired goods and services, as well as what qualifications Congress could require prospective bidders for such contracts to meet.

The incursion into Congress' turf was significant, but the GATT's dispute resolution and enforcement systems did not make these new rules truly binding on signatory countries. At that time, the GATT utilized a dispute-settlement procedure – fleshed out over decades of practice – that mediated inter-country conflicts. Panels convened under this dispute practice were comprised of trade experts, who analyzed challenged laws. The GATT Tokyo Round "Technical Barriers to Trade" and "Procurement" Codes both included similar panel systems. But national governments had more power under these systems than they do under the WTO today. For instance, the pre-1994 GATT procedures included the standard diplomatic safeguard of requiring all members' consensus before taking punitive measures or other transformative actions. So if a member country strongly objected to a GATT panel's conclusion that its laws violated GATT rules, or to orders that it change a domestic law, that country could block adoption of such a ruling. Thus, it could determine when the downsides of not complying with a ruling outweighed other national interests, and could avoid trade sanctions for maintaining GATT-inconsistent policies.[145]

While the Fast Track aspect of the 1974 trade package was used both to extend enormously the scope of "trade"-agreement jurisdiction and to ignore Congress' instructions regarding what should and should not be in the next GATT round, the other aspects of the 1974 trade

---

145. Jackson, 1997, at 163-168.

package came largely to naught. For instance, the Ford and Carter administrations did not utilize the broad import-surcharge authority provided in the package, and instead focused on a "jawboning" strategy of talking down the dollar and talking up foreign demand for U.S. exports. This approach failed to close the growing trade deficit.[146]

In the congressional mock markups on the Tokyo Round implementing legislation, labor-union representatives urged that procurement and other non-tariff issues be taken out of the agreement.[147] Human rights and religious groups urged the Carter administration to make good on its commitment to include labor rights in the GATT and focus on poor-country development.[148] And, once again, congressional concerns about the use of trade agreements by the executive branch to intrude on Congress' jurisdiction were dismissed. For instance, on the House floor, a number of congressmembers expressed concern about the new authority for the president to waive "Buy American" rules for federal procurement. Rep. Charles Vanik (D-Ohio) – the chair of the Ways & Means trade subcommittee – deflected the jurisdictional issue by talking instead about the export opportunities in foreign procurement markets, or by raising the exceptions to the broad waiver authority, such as for certain Defense Department (DOD) contracts. Witness this colloquy, which did little to clarify what was actually at stake:

> Rep. John Ashbrook (R-Ohio): *Can the gentleman visualize any United States standard, anything that relates to health, safety, industrial, or agricultural, that in some way is not affected by this bill that could be altered, waiver or otherwise shaped by GATT or someone outside?*
>
> Vanik: *I do not believe that there is anything in this bill that would decrease or diminish or detract from any U.S. standard.*
>
> Ashbrook: *Or any other U.S. statute?*
>
> Vanik: *Nothing that I can see in this legislation.*

---

146. Biven, 2002, at 120 and 178.
147. WM, 1979, at 441.
148. WM, 1979, at 626 and 633.

Ashbrook: *Well, in the first place, we know, I would remind my friend that that is not so. Specifically… the president can waive what we know to be the 'Buy America' law.*

Vanik: *That does not apply to DOD at all.*

Ashbrook: *Well, I did not say DOD. Is the gentleman saying that the president cannot waive the Buy America Act?*

Vanik: *He cannot waive it. It does not apply at all to DOD. The president has no power by this bill to do that…*

Rep. Robert Bauman (R-Md.): *Earlier today I asked [Vanik] this very question, and the gentleman told me there was no authority in this act that would allow the president to waive the Buy America Act… [but] this act provides him with new power that he never had before…*

Ashbrook: *I myself look upon it as dropping a lot of time bombs, a lot of trip wires, setting up a lot of minefields … I intend to vote against this bill. I think we have gone far beyond anything necessary and have not protected our own interests adequately.*

The chairman of the Government Operations Committee, which had jurisdiction over procurement, expressed concern that the implementing legislation for the Tokyo Round gave the president too much waiver authority and that he would not have to come back to Congress for approval of any future gutting of "Buy American" rules. It is worth noting that the chairman was not seeking to alter the terms of the Tokyo Round agreement. Rather, at issue was the executive branch using Fast Track to establish new and ongoing authority to alter unilaterally policies clearly under Congress' remit. But he – like other members concerned about executive branch encroachments – was forbidden from amending the legislation due to Fast Track rules.

The resulting Trade Agreement Act of 1979 implemented the Tokyo Round and extended Fast Track authority until 1988.[149] Interestingly, the 1979 Act was not a vote on congressional approval of the

149. Public Law 96-39 § 1101.

underlying GATT agreement, which was still only under provisional acceptance by the United States.[150] Also, the new grant of Fast Track which was included in the bill explicitly required that, if the president determined that GATT or other trade pacts required further changes in U.S. statutes, he would have to request Congress to consider such changes through normal congressional procedures, and give the gatekeeper committees 30 days advance notice before sending up the suggested statutory changes to Congress.[151] The 1979 legislation passed almost unanimously in both houses.[152]

c. Fast Tracking the Continuing Incursion on Congress' Authority, 1980-1988

President Ronald Reagan came to office inheriting the eight-year delegation of Fast Track authority passed in the 1979 Act. At the time, the trade deficit was increasing and Congress was responding with various proposals to limit imports, especially from developing countries. Legislation authorizing the Generalized System of Preferences (GSP), a system providing special low tariffs to imports from developing countries, was expiring, and pressure was building to exempt richer-country beneficiaries (such as Hong Kong, Taiwan and South Korea) from continuing in the program.[153] At the same time, Reagan's advisors convinced him to take trade actions that intervened in the free market. This included currency-market interventions and the negotiation of voluntary export restraints, including an agreement with Japan limiting the number of cars that could be sent to the United States. Such actions, similar to those taken by Nixon, conflicted with Reagan's deregulatory philosophy.

As an array of trade bills consumed much of Congress' attention, the Reagan administration focused on the GATT. Reagan faced considerable congressional opposition to many of his non-trade domestic legislative initiatives. However, key elements of Reagan's non-trade

---

150. Jackson, Louis and Matsushita, 1982, at 345.
151. Public Law 96-39 § 3(c).
152. Passed House on July 11, 1979 by a 395-7 margin (D: 247-5; R: 148-2). Passed Senate on July 23, 1979 by a 90-4 margin (D: 52-3; R: 38-1).
153. Destler, 2005, at 83-88, and 115-129.

agenda that were being thwarted in the context of U.S. public and congressional debate found a perfect home in the context of obscure international negotiations. The Uruguay Round of GATT talks (launched in 1986 in Punta del Este, Uruguay) provided a suitable delivery mechanism.[154] Reagan administration officials – led by USTR official Geza Feketekuty – played a leading role in formulating a Uruguay Round agenda that focused on the administration's push to limit governments' role in regulating the service sector, setting food and product safety rules, and more.[155]

It is interesting to consider how Fast Track enabled this strategy of circumventing Congress with respect to domestic policy matters that were subject to heated debate at home. Perhaps because Congress had no experience of such expansive back-door diplomatic legislating via trade agreements, the Reagan administration strategy went largely unnoticed. And, even if it had been noticed, Fast Track strictly limited Congress' role in the process. However, decades later, congressional Republicans were up in arms against the prospect of a president using trade negotiations to institute new labor rights obligations to which the United States would be bound. The Fast Track delegation passed in 2002 included negotiating objectives to limit such measures in future agreements. Somewhat ironically, thanks to the structure of Fast Track, which makes such congressional objectives unenforceable, congressional Republicans found themselves facing Fast Tracked votes on trade agreements with Peru, Korea, Colombia and Panama that included entire chapters on labor rights and the most robust labor standards of any past U.S. trade agreement.

With respect to the Reagan administration's agenda for GATT Uruguay Round negotiations, there was ample domestic and international opposition to the notion that countries' service-sector or investment regulations should be set internationally, much less by trade negotiators whose experience was largely limited to tariffs, quotas and the procurement issues from the 1970s Tokyo Round. It was thus of ex-

---

154. Wallach and Woodall, 2004, at 3.
155. Drake and Nicolaidis, 1992, at 52. One Feketekuty ally told the *Chicago Tribune* in 1980, just days after Reagan's election victory: "A lot of services that have traditionally been done by the government, such as education, and social services, may become something that we'll have to deal with in international commerce." Tefft, 1980.

treme importance to Reagan that he find a legislative vehicle to obtain new authority to further expand the scope of "trade" negotiations that would avoid intense congressional scrutiny and potential criticisms while obtaining maximum legislative support. As it turned out, a bill that had been kicking around Congress since 1983 authorizing negotiation of an FTA with Israel – which had 163 House cosponsors and was supported primarily on foreign-policy grounds – proved to be the perfect option. Several of the trade bills then under consideration in Congress, including some trade balancing measures and the GSP reauthorization, were combined into a package that became the Trade and Tariff Act of 1984 [156]

In order to overcome House opposition to the GSP and non-trade measures, the Senate Finance Committee reported out a bill (H.R. 3398) that combined these elements with authorization for Israel FTA negotiations. On September 20, 1984, the bill passed the Senate by a 96-0 vote. Because the House had not passed any of the component legislation, Ways & Means reported out four separate bills, and passed each of them on October 3. This was orchestrated by Chair Dan Rostenkowski (D-Ill.), who had taken Wilbur Mills' place as trade dealmaker-in-chief. Among the four bills was a new extension of Fast Track (H.R. 5377), which the House passed on a 416-6 vote. After a conference to resolve the differences, a week later the final measure (H.R. 3398) passed the House on a 386-1 vote on October 9, 1984 and passed the Senate on a voice vote the same day.

Largely flying under the radar, the 1984 Trade and Tariff Act dramatically expanded the subject matter and the types of agreements that the president was authorized to negotiate. Title III of the Act authorized the president to collect information on (and enter into agreements related to the elimination of) "barriers to international trade in services" and "the trade distortive effects of certain investment-related measures." Service and investment barriers were defined as denial of "national treatment and restrictions on the establishment" of service operations and investments; "foreign industrial policies;" "export performance requirements;" and "direct or indirect restrictions

---

156. Destler, 2005, at 84.

on the transfer of information into, or out of" a given country. The Commerce Department was also authorized to collect information on other governments' failures to enforce copyrights and patents, which were identified as barriers to trade (even though patent monopolies are deemed a rent-seeking protection that distorts free markets in standard economics theory).[157]

The 1984 Fast Track delegation also included a new delegation of authority for the president to negotiate and enter into bilateral FTAs across a wide range of tariff and non-tariff matters. While negotiations with Israel were greenlighted by the statute, the gatekeeper committees were to be given an additional 60-day notice in addition to the required 90-day notice before trade agreements with other countries were signed. If the executive failed to provide such notice, the proposed pact would not receive Fast Track treatment. Moreover, under the 1984 Act, the gatekeeper committees could take an agreement off the Fast Track for any reason at all during that 60-day period.[158] During the debate over an FTA with Canada, Sen. Max Baucus (D-Mont.) catapulted to prominence on the trade issue by becoming the ringleader of an effort to force administration action on Asian trade issues. His tactic? Threatening to use the 1984 Act's disapproval resolution to withhold use of Fast Track for the Canada pact. In the end, the administration cut side deals with a variety of senators and Fast Track was applied to the Canada FTA.[159]

As one legal scholar noted in 1986, the 1984 disapproval provision "dramatically expanded the influence of the House Ways & Means Committee and the Senate Finance Committee vis-à-vis the rest of Congress."[160] (However, the broad procedure allowing Fast Track disapproval by gatekeeper committees was subsequently removed during the 1988 Fast Track, which instead included a narrow disapproval resolution limited to situations in which the executive failed to give notice or properly consult with Congress.[161]) While the addition of

---

157. Public Law 98-573 §§ 301-308.
158. Public Law 98-578 § 401(a)(4)(B).
159. Koh, 1986, at 1214-1221.
160. Koh, 1986, at 1213.
161. See Forbes, 2008, for more detail on disapproval resolutions.

any Fast Track disapproval resolution sounded like an improvement in Congress' relative power compared to the original Fast Track process (and the broad mechanism in the 1984 Act *did* provide leverage in its one threatened use), the post-1988 procedural disapproval resolution provisions meant little in practical terms. As long as the executive branch went through the motions of notifying Congress, neither the gatekeeper committees nor Congress as a whole retained any role in selecting negotiating-partner countries or controlling the content of agreements.

The Israel FTA, passed in 1985, was modest in scope by today's standards. The Canada FTA, however, included chapters and provisions related to investment, financial regulation, and intellectual property – a greatly expanded scope from the reciprocal tariff agreements of the past.[162] The Reagan administration rushed negotiations on the Canada pact to official completion in late 1987, so that Congress could be notified 90 days before a planned signing on January 2, 1988 – the very last day before the Fast Track delegation expired. However, according to trade analyst I.M. Destler: "To legislators' annoyance, and contrary to the law's intent, major substantive provisions of the agreement were defined in the period *between* the October notification and the January signing."[163] Under Fast Track's terms, Congress retained no mechanism to counter this abuse.

Even though its scope expanded beyond any past trade agreement, the 1988 Canada-U.S. FTA did not draw much attention in the United States beyond agricultural-state representatives. Few in Congress were even aware of its many non-tariff provisions. In Canada, the pact, which threatened to drag stronger Canadian environmental and safety laws down to U.S. levels, generated passionate grassroots opposition and became a major national political issue.[164]

---

162. For instance, the Canada-U.S. FTA required that Canada export a fixed percentage of oil to the United States, even if Canada experiences an energy shortage. See Laxer and Dillon, 2008, at 12.
163. Destler, 2005, at 96.
164. Barlow, 1998, at 99.

d. Failure of Attempts to Reform Fast Track, 1988-1994[165]

As the Reagan era drew to an end, the U.S. trade deficit continued to grow and manufacturing jobs started to decline. Congress began demanding a return to import surcharges. Reagan partially stifled these demands by negotiating the 1985 Plaza Accords, an international agreement to allow the dollar to depreciate against other currencies,[166] and by extending voluntary export restraint agreements in which trade partners agreed to limit steel exports to the United States.

But deindustrialization continued, and the Democratic Congress saw a new opening to address the issue through the 1988 expiration of Fast Track. In particular, some in Congress sought to condition a new delegation of trade authority on the insertion of labor standards into trade pacts, and on an enhanced Section 301 process that could pressure trade partners such as Japan for more market access.[167] The result: the Omnibus Trade and Competitiveness Act of 1988.

The 1988 Act was unique in the history of Fast Track delegations, in that the president did not initiate a request for new authority. In fact, Reagan eventually demonstrated his displeasure by vetoing the bill passed by Congress. The version of the bill that Reagan vetoed passed twice in each chamber – once in initial form, once in conferenced form.

While the House voted to override the president's veto, the Senate was unable to do so. Ultimately, Rostenkowski brokered a compromise bill that removed provisions opposed by Reagan that would give workers advance notice if their plant were closing. (Congress passed the so-

---

165. For the following sections, we occasionally draw on our own firsthand experiences in addition to the cited primary and secondary sources. One of us played a leading role in trade legislative debates since 1990; the other since 2004.

166. Bradsher, 2004; Farnsworth, 1985a; Farnsworth, 1985b.

167. Section 301 refers to provisions of the Trade Act under which "the United States may impose trade sanctions against foreign countries that maintain acts, policies and practices that violate, or deny U.S. rights or benefits under, trade agreements, or are unjustifiable, unreasonable or discriminatory and burden or restrict U.S. commerce." The provision allowed the USTR to initiate an investigation of the trade practices of another country, either on its own initiative, or upon the request of a U.S. citizen. The WTO undermined the use of such unilateral trade enforcement mechanisms, which is ironic, since the WTO was negotiated and approved under the very same 1988 Fast Track bill that initiated the Section 301 process. For discussion of trade offs on market access mechanisms in the 1988 bill versus the 2001 bill, see "Zoellick Signals Fast-Track Link To U.S.-Jordan Trade Deal," *Inside U.S. Trade*, March 2, 2001.

called "WARN Act" as stand-alone legislation that later became law.)[168] The final vote on that compromise bill, which Reagan signed, flipped the tables on the traditional trade divisions in Congress, with those who had been critical of current trade policies, such as Reps. Byron Dorgan (D-N.D.) and Marcy Kaptur (D-Ohio) supporting the bill, and those who supported the existing policies, like Sen. John McCain (R-Ariz.) and Reps. Newt Gingrich (R-Ga.), Tom DeLay (R-Texas) and Phil Crane (R-Ill.), voting against it.[169]

Like the Nixon-Mills pair before them and the Bush-Thomas pair after them, President Ronald Reagan (pictured in center) and Chair Dan Rostenkowski (left) formed a partnership to get Fast Track through Congress and signed into law. Rostenkowski also partnered on Fast Track with presidents George H.W. Bush and Bill Clinton. Rostenkowski's political career ended in 1994 after a two-year investigation by the Justice Department which led to an indictment on corruption charges for his role in the House post office scandal. He was forced to step down from all congressional leadership positions. In elections later that year, Rostenkowski lost his seat and retired from political life.[170]

---

168. Destler, 2005, at 91-96.

169. The stronger version – H.R. 3 – passed the House three times: on a 290-137 vote on April 30, 1987; on a conference vote of 312-107 on April 21, 1988; and on a veto override of 308-113 on May 24. The bill passed in the Senate twice, by a 71-27 margin on July 21, 1987, by a 63-36 margin in the conference vote on April 27, 1988. On June 8, the Senate failed to override Reagan on a 61-37 vote, thus failing to get a two-thirds majority. The House passed a watered down version (H.R. 4848) by a 376-45 margin on July 13, (D: 243-4; R: 133-41), and the Senate approved the bill by an 85-11 margin on Aug. 3, 1988 (D: 50-1; R: 35-10). The bill, titled the Omnibus Trade and Competitiveness Act, became Public Law 100-418, 102 Stat. 1107.

170. Charges against Rostenkowski included keeping "ghost" employees on his payroll, using congressional funds to buy gifts for friends, using taxpayer funds to pay for vehicles used for personal transportation and trading-in officially purchased stamps for cash at the House post office. The stamps-for-cash charges were dismissed on the recommendation of the prosecutor. In 1996, Rostenkowski pleaded guilty to reduced charges of mail fraud. He served 15 months in federal prison. Rostenkowski was pardoned in December 2000 by President Clinton in one of his last acts in office.

Despite the inclusion of labor rights in its principal negotiating objectives,[171] this grant of Fast Track produced NAFTA and facilitated much of the Uruguay Round negotiations – neither of which contained labor standards. (President Clinton added a labor side agreement with extremely limited enforceability to NAFTA a year after President George H.W. Bush signed the actual NAFTA text.) Both NAFTA and the Uruguay Round's WTO exploded past trade agreement boundaries to include a wide array of non-trade policy constraints and obligations. Members of Congress and advocates grew increasingly frustrated as their "model" delegation authority had been twisted to produce "trade" agreements in which real trade policy occupied a minority position among hundreds of pages of non-trade provisions. A closer look would have revealed that in addition to adding labor rights, Rostenkowski's bill had only expanded on Reagan's 1984 Fast Track in regards to authorizing the executive branch to set investment, services, intellectual property and other non-trade policies through trade negotiations.[172]

Congress' interest was particularly piqued when President George H.W. Bush gave notice to Congress in February 1991 of his intent to use Fast Track to negotiate a North American Free Trade Agreement (NAFTA) that expanded on the U.S.-Canada FTA's scope and added Mexico. Mexico's per-capita income at the time was 10 to 15 percent of U.S. levels, and environmental, sanitation and food-safety conditions in Mexico were a cause of worry sufficient to generate State Department travel advisories for visiting Americans.[173]

Meanwhile, a complete Uruguay Round draft text leaked. The new text showed the stunning scope of the talks, which focused *mainly* on non-tariff issues and the setting of globally binding constraints on an array of policies previously under the sole jurisdiction of domestic national and state legislatures. This new breadth included limits on

---

171. *See* Omnibus Trade and Competitiveness Act of 1988 § 1101(b), 102 Stat. at 1121-25. Section 1101(b) lays out negotiating objectives with section 1101(b)(14) listing as principal U.S. negotiating objectives: (A) to promote respect for worker rights; (B) to secure a review of the relationship of worker rights to GATT articles, objectives, and related instruments with a view to ensuring that benefits of the trading system are available to all workers; and (C) to adopt, as a principle of GATT, that the denial of worker rights should not be a means for a country or its industries to gain competitive advantage in international trade.
172. Public Law 100-418 § 1101.
173. MacArthur, 2000, at 103-125; Faux, 2006, at 36; and Salas, 2006.

the regulation of service-sector firms operating within a country, patent and copyright law, immigration policy and more. The text also included a proposal to establish a new global commerce agency then called the "Multilateral Trade Organization" (MTO), under which GATT and a dozen new agreements would be subsumed. Fighting against overwhelming congressional disbelief that a "trade" agreement could implicate such issues or enter the United States into a new international organization without a treaty vote, advocates representing conservative views as well as consumer and environmental groups joined labor in trying to draw congressional attention to the proposal. Then, in March 1991, a GATT tribunal issued a ruling against the U.S. Marine Mammal Protection Act, the law that forbid U.S. sale of tuna fish caught with purse seine nets, a method that had led to high rates of dolphin death. The law had been passed after a nationwide campaign by schoolchildren, and the policy had broad bipartisan support. The case, dubbed "GATTzilla v. Flipper" by Fast Track opponents, became Exhibit #1 in the threats posed by over-reaching international commercial rules and tribunals, undermining non-trade policy.[174]

The disenchantment in Congress was palpable. After the NAFTA announcement, growing numbers of members became increasingly angry about their inability to control executive branch selection of countries with which to the U.S. might initiate trade negotiations. It was also becoming increasingly clear that executive-branch negotiators were ignoring those congressional negotiating objectives that did not comport with their own goals, while adding aspects to pacts – such as the MTO, later renamed the WTO – never contemplated by Congress. As the NAFTA and GATT Uruguay Round talks continued, many in Congress saw themselves placed in the position of having to agree to numerous objectionable non-trade provisions in the pacts (plus various totally unrelated provisions tucked into the implementing legislation),[175] in order to support non-objectionable provisions that

---

174. Dunne, 1992; Wallach and Woodall, 2004, at 4; Jackson, 1992, at 1250-1253.
175. For instance, the Uruguay Round Agreements Act (URAA) sections 771-778 included changes to the Pension Benefit Guarantee Corporation statute that changed the way defined benefit plans must calculate the lump-sum value of a participant's vested accrued benefit. Sections 761-764 changed other aspects of the Employee Retirement Income Security Act (ERISA). Section 801 of the URAA also amended the Communications Act regarding what were called pioneer spectrum preferences. The URAA also directed the FCC to award licenses within fifteen days to certain applicants, including one related to a newspaper editorializing heavily for congressional passage of the bill.

actually concerned trade expansion. This growing dismay led to the end of wide bipartisan support for Fast Track.

One concrete expression of this ire was the introduction of the first resolution of disapproval for a Fast Track extension. The 1988 Fast Track was written so that it would run until 1991 and then continue on until 1993, unless Congress passed a resolution of disapproval to stop the extension past 1991. Such an extension disapproval resolution could be introduced by any member of Congress, and would enjoy a privileged guaranteed vote.[176] In March 1991, Rep. Dorgan and Sen. Ernest Hollings (D-S.C.) invoked this provision to lead a majority of Democrats in voting to discontinue the grant of Fast Track.[177] In I.M. Destler's words:

> "At this time the issue could have been killed in committee
> – the law provided that a fast-track disapproval resolution
> could reach the House or Senate floor only if the requisite
> committee(s) approved. But committee and chamber leaders
> quickly decided that burial in committee, while perfectly legal,
> would be viewed as politically egregious and thus discredit
> both the procedures and any agreements reached thereunder.
> Disapproval resolutions would have to go to both floors, and
> be voted up or down there."[178]

The Ways & Means and Finance committees thus reported out the resolutions, although with the recommendation that they be rejected by the Congress as a whole. (The House committee's negative recommendation passed 27-9, and the Senate committee's was 15-3.) Nonetheless, the actual House floor vote on the extension disapproval resolution was somewhat close – 192-231. The resolution failed to obtain a majority thanks in part to a partnership between Republican President Bush and the Democratic chairs of the gatekeeper

---

176. Omnibus Trade and Competitiveness At of 1988, P.L. 100-418, § 1103 (b)(5). For more information on disapproval resolutions, see Forbes, 2008.
177. H. Res. 101, the Dorgan disapproval in the House, received 192 votes for (170 Democrats, 21 Republicans and one independent), and 231 votes against (91 Democrats, and 140 Republicans). The Hollings Senate resolution attracted 36 votes (31 Democrats and 5 Republicans), with 59 nay votes (23 Democrats and 36 Republicans).
178. Destler, 2005, at 98.

committees. Rostenkowski and his Senate counterpart Lloyd Bentsen (D-Tex.) got Bush to promise a non-binding "action plan" on NAFTA labor and environmental issues in return for committee opposition to the Dorgan-Hollings resolutions.[179] As a face-saving measure, members were allowed to let off steam by voting the same day for a non-binding "sense of the Congress" resolution (H. Res. 146) on what should be and what should not be in NAFTA and the WTO.[180] (In 2005, Dorgan – later elected to the Senate – introduced an extension disapproval resolution under the 2002 Fast Track. This time, the Finance Committee simply bottled it up and refused to let the measure go to the floor.)[181]

Congressional exasperation with pacts negotiated under Fast Track grew in 1992. The previous year's GATT ruling against the popular U.S. dolphin protection law was the first in a series of trade pact tribunal rulings that would be issued against U.S. non-trade laws under NAFTA and WTO. Starting with that first tuna-dolphin decision, each of these rulings began to awaken members of Congress to the ways in which trade agreements were invading Congress' policymaking space.

Yet, with Fast Track in place, executive branch negotiators were largely shielded from having to respond to the growing congressional concerns about the overreaching provisions of various pacts. In yet another attempt to reinsert Congress in a formative role in deciding trade agreement's substantive rules, House Democrats Henry Waxman (D-Cal.) and Richard Gephardt (D-Mo.) introduced in 1992 a resolution regarding negotiating objectives for the Uruguay Round and NAFTA (H. Con. Res 246):

> "The Congress calls upon the President to initiate and complete negotiations, as part of the current Uruguay Round GATT talk, to make the GATT compatible with the Marine Mammal Protection Act and other United States health, safety, labor, and environmental laws, including those laws that are designed to

---

179. Carrier, 1996, at 712.
180. Destler, 2005, at 99-101.
181. S. Res. 100, introduced April 6, 2005.

protect the environment outside the geographic borders of the United States.

The Congress will not approve legislation to implement any trade agreement (including the Uruguay Round of the GATT and the United States-Mexico Free Trade Agreement) if such agreement jeopardizes United States health, safety, labor, or environmental laws (including the Federal Food, Drug, and Cosmetic Act and the Clean Air Act)."

Ways & Means Chair Rostenkowski refused to mark up the resolution and then-House Speaker Tom Foley (D-Wash.) refused to schedule it on the suspension calendar. However, when a majority of House members had cosponsored the measure and talk about a discharge petition began, a vote was scheduled on the eve of congressional recess in 1992. After battling the resolution for months, its strongest Democratic opponents - eager to blur distinctions that could later become electoral liabilities – urged all members to support it and it passed on August 7 by a nearly party-line vote of 246-172.[182] Yet, executive branch negotiators, working behind the shield of Fast Track, ignored the measure and proceeded with their own agenda. After providing Congress with the required notice, shortly before leaving office President Bush signed the completed NAFTA text.

The Clinton administration arrived in 1993 with NAFTA negotiated and signed by the Bush administration and ready to go to Congress under Fast Track. But in Geneva, the GATT talks were bogged down over agricultural issues and opposition by many countries to the expansive service-sector, investment, procurement and intellectual-property aspects of the proposed deal.[183] The negotiations were heading towards establishing a new global commerce agency, the WTO, which would provide much stronger enforcement of GATT's rules, and transform the pact's contracting parties into members of a new international organization with ongoing negotiating remit. These plans also drew considerable concern from many countries as well as

---

182. Democrats provided the 246 yes votes. Three Democrats joined 169 GOP to vote no. Several key Ways & Means Democratic members abstained from voting.
183. Raghavan, 1990a.

from members of the U.S. Congress concerned with safeguarding U.S. sovereignty.[184]

Rather than altering these pacts, the Clinton administration made passing NAFTA a top priority,[185] and launched an intense campaign against the majority of the Democratic base groups that had just worked to elect him. The NAFTA campaign squandered the new president's political capital for passing the health-care reform proposals that had been a highlight of his campaign.[186] The Clinton administration then pushed for passage of a short Fast Track extension specifically to allow completion of the Uruguay Round.[187]

The sudden encroachment of "trade" agreements into an array of non-trade domestic policy issues drew the attentions of diverse new constituencies, from right-leaning sovereignty defenders to centrist small business and consumer rights advocates to left-leaning environmentalists. The 1993 votes on NAFTA and the 1994 vote on the WTO attracted a very determined and broad-based opposition. This included hundreds of advocacy groups never before involved in a trade fight.

Many in Congress dismissed these groups' concerns. Massive campaigns by the Clinton administration (and by the Mexican government with respect to NAFTA) and diverse commercial interests who supported aspects of the pacts characterized their opponents as uninformed, loopy and protectionist.[188] Given that no past trade agreement had, for instance, increased monopoly protections for pharmaceutical companies, allowed foreign corporations to skirt U.S. courts to sue the U.S. government for cash compensation, or required Congress to

---

184. According to Raghavan: "If the Industrialized Countries have their way, the Brussels Ministerial meeting of the Uruguay Round Trade Negotiations Committee (TNC) is to take steps to establish a Multilateral Trade Organization (MTO) that would effectively take over the work of the rest of the UN system in areas covered by the Uruguay Round negotiations… The idea of converting GATT into the ITO was flagged by the EC early this year…The Group of 77 at UNCTAD and elsewhere came out against converting GATT into the ITO, whereupon the EC put forward the idea of an MTO which in name would be different from the ITO but in practice would amount to the same thing." See Raghavan, 1990b.
185. IUT, 1993.
186. Wilentz, 2008, at 335.
187. The bill (H.R. 1876) passed the House by a 295-126 margin June 22, 1993 (Democrats: 145-102; Republicans 150-23), and the Senate by a 76-16 margin on June 30, 1993. It became Public Law 103-49.
188. MacArthur, 2000, at 233.

conform wide swaths of law unrelated to trade to its terms, many in Congress simply did not believe the critics who raised these issues.

And with Fast Track limiting normal committee procedures, relatively few hearings were held on these aspects of the agreement. Most in Congress understood NAFTA and the WTO to be *trade* agreements, not broader sets of policy proposals directly affecting their jurisdiction and thus requiring their special concern or attention. Indeed, during the WTO debate, it came out that hardly any members of Congress had read the Uruguay Round agreements.[189] The congresspeople outside the gatekeeper committees who did prioritize the NAFTA and WTO debates largely focused on job-related or industry-specific concerns. Some members of Congress claimed that it would be inappropriate – despite their concerns with the legislation – to reject an agreement that had taken the president years to negotiate. Still other fence sitters in the NAFTA battle were amenable to what the Center for Public Integrity called an "orgy of dealmaking" on unrelated issues that characterized the Clinton administration's legislative approach.[190]

Even ardent defenders of Fast Track recognized that NAFTA and the WTO had revealed Fast Track's enormous discretion for "diplomatic legislating" by the executive branch. One such analyst, Yale Law School Professor Harold Koh, later to become the Legal Adviser of the Department of State under the Obama administration, conceded that: "Fast Track gives the President greater freedom to shape trade agreements to his programmatic agenda than would otherwise be possible under ordinary legislative process."[191] In November 1993, Congress passed NAFTA by a 234-200 vote. This was the closest trade-agreement vote in modern history, and included 102 Democrats voting for NAFTA, in part to support their new president.[192]

---

189. Skidmore, 1994. John Jackson pointed out that the WTO's "26,000 pages of text, schedule commitments, and other matters... is a record for its length." See Jackson, 1997, at 166.
190. Lewis, 1993; Tucker, Wu and Prorok, 2005.
191. Koh, 1992, at 171.
192. The NAFTA implementing bill, H.R. 3450, passed the House November 13, 1993 by 234-200 (D: 102-156; R: 132-43) and the Senate on November 20, 1993 by 61-38. It became Public Law 103-182.

Meanwhile, the Clinton administration had begun bilateral meetings with European trade officials to try to resolve the agricultural issues that had thwarted agreement by the two major GATT powers on the Uruguay Round. And, the White House started to air the idea of expanding NAFTA to additional countries in the Americas. Chile signaled interest in being the next U.S. FTA partner. Given the administration had no Fast Track authority at the time, some in Congress worked to get ahead of the foreseeable next request for Fast Track to try to reform the process. Prominent NAFTA opponent and House Democratic Majority Leader Richard Gephardt, and one of NAFTA's leading proponents, Rep. Bill Richardson (D-N.M), submitted a bill, H.R. 4375, the "Chile Free Trade Agreement Negotiating Act of 1994"in May 1994.[193] Both had supported the Fast Track extension in 1991.

The purpose of the legislation, which was cosponsored by current Ways & Means Ranking member Sander Levin (D-Mich.) was: "To provide negotiating authority for a trade agreement with Chile, but to apply fast track procedures only to such an agreement that contains certain provisions relating to worker rights and the environment." The proposal sought to address one of the most problematic aspects of Fast Track – the ability of administration negotiators to ignore Congress' negotiating objectives with impunity. The proposal did this by requiring that a Chile FTA implementing legislation could only obtain Fast Track's special congressional consideration floor rules if the Chile FTA itself met certain objectives. This included FTA provisions "requiring the parties to adhere to internationally recognized worker rights (as defined in section 502(a)(4) of the Trade Act of 1974)…to enforce their environmental laws and to take steps to adopt appropriate higher environmental standards." The pact also included "dispute resolution mechanisms to enforce effectively" those requirements.

The proposal provided that at the time the implementing bill was submitted, the president had to certify to the Congress that the

---

193. H.R. 4375 Text of bill available at http://www.gpo.gov/fdsys/pkg/BILLS-103hr4375ih/pdf/
BILLS-103hr4375ih.pdf

objectives had been met. And, it provided a 15 day window for the House Rules Committee or the Senate Committee on Rules and Administration to disapprove the President's certification, which would result in Fast Track's special floor rules not being applied. Relative to past Fast Track bills, the proposal would have provided Congress with more leverage over negotiators, in that it created liabilities if Congress' objectives were not met. Instead of a guaranteed vote within 90 days, the president could face the prospect that the trade agreement's implementing bill would not be taken up by Congress, or if it was that it would be subject to normal floor procedures, including various Senate supermajority cloture votes.

The hitch with this approach was that it empowered the president, rather than Congress, to determine if Congress' objectives had been met. And, it did so at a late stage in the process. The political realities of that moment provided a solution to the first problem. Rep. David Bonior (D-Mich.), a passionate opponent of NAFTA and Fast Track, was the chairman of the House Rules Committee. Bonior, who had led the House whipping operation against both measures, was deeply committed to changing the substance of U.S. trade agreements and the negotiating and approval process. He could be relied upon to disapprove a Clinton administration certification if in fact the agreement did not meet the bill's criteria.

But the timing issue remained. The Fast Track delegation included the right for the President to *sign* and *enter into* agreements *before* Congress voted. Thus the required labor and environmental provisions would have been completed (or not) well before the proposal provided Congress with its lever for accountability, which would come upon submission of a signed Chile FTA's implementing bill to Congress. As a result, the juncture when the president and Congress could come to a disagreement about whether the objectives had been met would be *after* the agreement was signed and sealed and the implementing bill submitted. The back-loading of Congress' role diminished the prospects that the proposal's goal – to ensure that trade agreements *included* robust labor and environmental provisions – would be achieved.

Even assuming that a disagreement between the president and Congress over fulfillment of negotiating objectives was a good faith difference of opinion, the mechanism would have left Congress in a difficult position. The president could shepherd the powerful arguments made in the past about damage to U.S. credibility and foreign relations if changes to a signed agreement were sought. Congress would be put on the defensive in this case, and face enormous pressure to proceed with consideration of the pact. And, even if the congressional Rules committees would strip the FTA of Fast Track application, efforts to use normal floor procedures to demand alterations to or disapprove of an agreement would face the same foreign policy arguments and pressures. In addition, if someone with the sensibilities of David Bonior was not chairing one of the congressional Rules committees, Congress' ability to retain control of the process would require those seeking specific FTA objectives to convince their leadership and the rules committees that the provisions the president certified were not sufficient. Unless those committees acted quickly, the default would be that Fast Track floor rules would apply.

While the Gephardt-Richardson proposal did not remedy these structural problems, it was a creative initiative that seized on circumstances specific to that political moment to try to rebalance the congressional-executive balance of power. Gephardt was uniquely positioned to increase the probability of success. Not only did he have a strong personal interest in reforming the terms of U.S. trade agreements and staff that closely followed trade negotiations, but as Majority Leader he scheduled House floor action and had considerable personal leverage to pressure administration trade officials to meet the objectives. If that failed, Bonior could act to reject the presidential certification. And, at the time executive branch negotiators and an array of congressional staff intensely engaged in the trade debate enjoyed a somewhat more cooperative relationship than that seen in recent years. Thus, acceptable labor and environmental provisions could have been informally pre-agreed, ameliorating the timing problem.

The proposal's core goal of increasing Congress' leverage over trade negotiators to comply with congressional negotiating objectives would become the basis for later Fast Track reform and replacement proposals. These included an initiative we will explore in the conclusion of this book that front-loaded Congress' role – by conditioning the delegation of congressional authority for the President *to sign and enter into* an agreement on a congressional certification or vote that Congress' objectives had been met.

The Gephardt-Richardson proposal was not passed and a year after the NAFTA vote in the 1994 midterm elections, Democrats lost control of Congress. Analysis of voting patterns revealed a large drop in white working class support for Democrats in key states, as voters irate about NAFTA turned to GOP appeals on social issues, or just stayed home.[194]

Meanwhile, before the 1994 election, a GATT tribunal had issued another ruling against a U.S. policy, the U.S. Corporate Average Fuel Efficiency (CAFE) standards. The winning claim was that some imported cars could be held to tougher standards than domestically-produced vehicles. The tribunal dismissed the fact that foreign auto makers' decisions to sell only their heavier, more expensive models in the United States were at the root of this alleged "discriminatory" outcome. Under GATT rules, the United States retained the right to ignore this ruling and the tuna-dolphin ruling without facing penalties.

Despite using this prerogative to keep domestic policies intact, the Democratic Party's final act in House leadership before a 12-year stint in the minority was passage of the Uruguay Round Agreements Implementation Act in a lame-duck session. The act established the WTO, creating the international commerce agency Truman had failed to get through Congress over 40 years before, at a moment of minimum political accountability.[195] Unlike the GATT, the WTO included binding enforcement through foreign tribunals empowered to impose trade sanctions if the United States did not alter its laws when the WTO so ordered.

---

194. Teixeira and Rogers, 2000; Engel and Jackson 1998.
195. The WTO implementing bill (H.R. 5110) passed the House on November 29, 1994 by 288-146 (D: 167-89; R: 121-56) and the Senate on December 1, 1994 by 76-24. It became Public Law 103-465.

The irony of the situation was uniquely bipartisan. The majority GOP support for the Uruguay Round Agreements Implementation Act created the WTO, an international body with perhaps the greatest power to require domestic enforcement of international law, despite the party's historic opposition to such international impositions. The law submitted the United States to the jurisdiction of foreign tribunals, despite consistent GOP outcry against such impositions to U.S. sovereignty. And, it eliminated Congress' authority to alter certain U.S. immigration policies, given that U.S. WTO obligations included a guarantee of a specific number of U.S. visas for foreign workers.

Meanwhile, in implementing the WTO, the Democratic Congress put in place an array of enforceable international rules that would be raised repeatedly to attack Democratic domestic priority policies relating to the environment, food safety and more. Indeed, one of the first cases filed before the new WTO international enforcement tribunal was a successful attack on U.S. gasoline cleanliness standards established in the Clean Air Act. (The WTO decision delivered a bipartisan sting, as once again, the winning claim was that the U.S. policy favored U.S. industry because the environmental goal had been implemented in a way that could result in more favorable treatment for domestic refiners relative to their foreign compotators.) After the non-enforcement of its GATT victory, Mexico then used the newly-created WTO to once again file its attack on the U.S. Marine Mammal Protection Act, won again, and this time obtained its sought-after elimination of the ban on U.S. sale of tuna caught using nets that kill dolphins.

NAFTA and the WTO Are Not Mainly About Tariffs or Trade

Agreements like NAFTA and the WTO contain hundreds of pages of non-tariff rules to which all signatory countries must conform their laws at all levels.[196] For instance, the WTO enforces 17 major agreements, only two of which are about trade in the traditional sense. NAFTA-style pacts contain various special investor privileges that provide foreign firms operating here favorable treatment relative to their domestic competitors and also reduce many of the risks and costs previously associated with U.S. firms relocating production to low-wage developing nations.[197] Among these are a minimum guaranteed standard of treatment for foreign investors, bans on performance requirements, and powerful enforcement systems that allow investors to avoid domestic courts. This "investor-state" enforcement system allows a foreign investor to directly "sue" governments before a World Bank or United Nations tribunal over domestic policies or government actions that it believes undermine its future expected profits or its expansive trade-pact rights, and to demand cash compensation from U.S. taxpayers for such losses.[198] Under the investor-state system of NAFTA-style deals, governments have already had to pay $365 million to foreign corporations for an array of domestic public health, energy, environmental and land use policies, and more than $14 billion remains in pending claims.[199]

Also, special WTO protections for pharmaceutical companies require signatory governments to provide them longer monopoly patents for medicines. The University of Minnesota found that complying with the WTO requirement to extend U.S. monopoly patent terms by three years (from the then 17-year term to a WTO-mandated 20-year term) would increase the cost of medicine for Americans by $8.6 billion over the next two decades. That figure only covers medicines that were under patent in 1994 (when Congress approved WTO membership), so the total cost today is much higher.[200] NAFTA and related FTAs extend these price-increasing monopoly protections even further.

---

196. For a comparative analysis of federal-subfederal consultation mechanisms on trade commitments under areas of shared jurisdiction, see Bottari and Wallach, 2008.
197. The WTO also contains investor protections that ban certain performance requirements and require national treatment once an investor is established.
198. Bottari and Wallach, 2005.
199. Public Citizen, "Table," 2013. For the full list of investor-state cases and claims under NAFTA-style deals, see http://www.citizen.org/documents/investor-state-chart.pdf.
200. Schondelmeyer, 1995, at 6-7. Inflation-adjusted using 2011 CPI-U-RS.

In addition, the Clinton administration bound certain U.S. immigration policies – including a guaranteed minimum of 65,000 H1-B visas per year for foreign workers to enter the United States[201] – with its WTO commitments. The United States was also obligated to conform domestic policies with respect to more than 100 U.S. service-sector categories to the terms of the WTO's service-sector agreement. This means that an array of U.S. land-use, financial, health-care, and climate policies are bound to comply with WTO mandates, and could be challenged if they do not conform to pact-established rules.[202] The WTO, NAFTA and the related FTAs also set limits on safety standards and inspection rates for imported food and products, even as these pacts include rules that increase the volume of imports.[203]

It is not merely a theoretical possibility that the constraints on domestic policy established in trade agreements can undermine non-trade policies and policy space. The ban on Internet gambling within U.S. territory was ruled to be a WTO violation by the organization's enforcement tribunals in 2004-05. U.S. Clean Air Act and Endangered Species Act regulations have been successfully attacked at the WTO and subsequently weakened. In 2011, the WTO ruled against three popular U.S. consumer protection policies: country-of-origin labels on meat, dolphin-safe labels on tuna and a ban on sweetly flavored cigarettes used to hook teenagers. WTO tribunals have ruled against challenged U.S. domestic laws over 91 per-cent of the time. [204] Under NAFTA, a tribunal ordered the United States to allow Mexico-domiciled trucks to have access to all U.S. roads, de-spite Mexico's weaker safety and environmental standards and less strin-gent commercial driver license requirements. Canadian extra-long and extra-heavy trucks also have similar rights thanks to NAFTA.[205] Beyond the WTO and NAFTA rulings themselves, mere threats of trade chal-lenges often have sufficed to chill policy proposals at home and abroad.[206]

In the end, the Bush I and Clinton administrations utilized Fast Track in the way that Nixon probably intended but was unable to accomplish in his own time. Over the course of the fifth regime, presidents bundled

---

201. Wallach and Tucker, 2006.
202. Tucker and Bottari, 2008.
203. Bottari, 2007; Tucker, Bottari and Pullen, 2007.
204. Public Citizen, 2013. Also see http://www.citizen.org/documents/
WTODisputesSummaryOnePagerwtables.pdf for win-loss ratios at the WTO.
205. Claybrook, 2007.
206. See Wallach and Woodall, 2004 and Bottari and Wallach, 2005 for instances of the chilling effect.

together their controversial trade *and domestic* priorities into "trade" agreements that were signed and locked before Congress had its first opportunity to vote on them, and written in trade jargon too complicated for all but the most determined to even decipher.

Approval of the agreements and lengthy implementing bills, altering swaths of domestic law, was then rammed through Congress on the legislative luge run established with Fast Track's suspension of normal committee proceedings and special floor consideration rules.

e. Fast Track is Dead, Part I, 1995-2001

Anger was increasing inside and outside of Congress at the invasion of domestic policy space by Fast Tracked "trade" deals. Critics raised two key concerns about how the Fast Track *process* was weakening the leverage of Congress and other groups not privileged to be appointed by the president to the formal advisory committees. First, Fast Track's structure had dramatically shifted the balance of power on a wide array of trade and non-trade policies to the executive branch. Instead of authorship by numerous members of Congress subject to some level of accountability by constituents (particularly in the House, with its two-year election cycle), policy was now made by *appointed* executive-branch staff who regularly revolved between industry and the administration. The president (who did face re-election pressures) could theoretically be held accountable. However, in practice, the concentration of trade policymaking power in one elected president – whom voters would judge on a vast array of policy decisions over four years – attenuated the accountability on specific trade decisions. Second, the Fast Tracked trade agreements were establishing and empowering supranational institutions – from the WTO itself to an array of WTO and NAFTA-recognized private-sector standardization bodies – which were shielded from democratic accountability altogether.[207]

---

207. Chorev, 2007; Engler, 2008, at 154.

> **As one WTO staff person admitted in a moment of candor, the WTO "is the place where governments collude in private against their domestic pressure groups."[208]**

In order to try to steer trade-agreement policymaking back towards trade and away from backdoor domestic non-trade policymaking, advocates created and strengthened cross-sectoral coalitions. These partnerships involved labor groups that had long been active on trade, but now teamed up with consumer, small business, farm, faith and environmental groups. These Fast Track critics utilized a comprehensive "inside-outside" strategy that combined lobbying with grassroots pressure. They also clarified that their goal was changing the "rules" or "model" of globalization, so that trade expansion could occur without sacrificing not only the principles and practice of democracy, but also the domestic, non-trade policies which democratic processes had created.[209]

In sum, the executive NAFTA-WTO overreach created a lasting political backlash against Fast Track. There were many dimensions to this resistance. Opposition to the Clinton trade agenda among congressional Democrats grew as the economic damage and political backlash from NAFTA and the WTO intensified. GOP congressional ire about Clinton's use of Fast Track to undermine sovereignty and to submit the U.S. to the jurisdiction of foreign tribunals only exacerbated intense Republican dislike and distrust of Clinton and a disinclination to grant him broad new powers. And the new cross-sectoral opposition coalitions were becoming increasingly effective, in no small part because the record of Fast Track-enabled trade agreements provided evidence to support the concerns they raised. All of these factors contributed to the Clinton administration being unable to obtain a delegation of Fast Track authority for the entire remainder of its tenure.

---

208. Jonquieres, 1998.
209. Shoch, 2000; Ehrlich 2008.

Trade Data Show that Fast Track Is Not Necessary For Trade Expansion

The Clinton administration is known for its major trade-expansion agenda, but it only had a delegation of Fast Track authority for the first two years of its eight-year period in office. Thus, Fast Track had relatively little to do with trade expansion *per se*. As already shown, the GATT – the single most important multilateral trade regime – was negotiated without the extraordinary procedural and non-trade-policymaking powers of Fast Track. By its own reckoning, the Clinton administration negotiated and passed 130 trade and investment agreements without Fast Track,[210] including the U.S.-Jordan Free Trade Agreement, which contained enhanced labor standards and was passed by almost universal acclaim under normal congressional floor procedures.[211] After Clinton lost Fast Track, from 1995 to 2000, trade expanded over 30 percent. As former Clinton administration USTR Charlene Barshefsky said in 2000, "if you look at our record on trade since 1995, I don't think the lack of Fast Track impeded our ability to achieve our major trade goals."[212]

Yet lack of trying does not explain why the Clinton administration was without presidential trade authority for six of its eight years.[213] After a failed effort to obtain Fast Track in 1995, Clinton worked in 1997 with GOP congressional leaders to develop a new Fast Track authorization bill. In contrast to the broad margins of passage for the 1979, 1984 and 1988 Fast Tracks, this bill faced fierce opposition. The administration, GOP congressional leaders and a broad corporate coalition lobbied fiercely for the bill. Although they were uncertain that they could garner support from a majority of Representatives, a vote was scheduled in the House. Speaker Newt Gingrich (R-Ga.) and the Clinton White House thought that actually starting the vote would create the maximum leverage for their efforts to obtain the last

---

210. This number comes from the Annual Trade Report of the USTR, which lists all trade and investment agreements in operation.
211. The Clinton administration negotiated the Jordan FTA, which Congress passed after he left office.
212. Quoted in Shapiro, 2006, at 79.
213. IUT, 1995a.

needed bloc of support. After a week's delay, the bill was brought to the House floor on November 9, 1997. Consideration of the measure started with the necessary precursor debate and vote on the rules for consideration of the underlying bill.

The climate on the House floor was volatile. Over the course of twelve hours of debate, the vote on the bill was pushed back repeatedly as the White House, GOP leaders and flocks of corporate lobbyists worked every angle in the Capitol's halls to build a majority. Ultimately, the Clinton administration finally asked the Republican leadership to pull down the Fast Track bill in the wee hours of November 10 after more than 80 percent of Democrats and many Republicans indicated they would oppose it.[214] Undoubtedly the prospect of Clinton suffering a high profile political defeat was tantalizing. GOP leaders complied with the Clinton request to pull the bill.[215] This was historic. Had the vote proceeded, Fast Track would have been defeated.

However, in 1998, congressional Republicans revived the Fast Track bill and brought it to a floor vote. It was defeated. In an unprecedented revolt against the formidable Republican Whip, Rep. Tom "The Hammer" DeLay (R-Texas), and Gingrich, 71 conservative GOP House members joined the 171 of 200 Democrats voting no.[216] The majority was comprised roughly of two camps. Despite fierce lobbying by corporate campaign donors and threats by Gingrich and DeLay, a sizeable bloc of GOP House members did not want to be seen as giving more authority to Clinton, whom they were lining up to impeach and volubly attacking in district events and in the media. The vast majority of Democrats, including many who had supported NAFTA, now also opposed Clinton's model of overreaching "trade" agreements and did not want to give him authority to do more of the same.

The political problems Fast Track caused for members of Congress were fundamental. Members who had voted for NAFTA and the WTO

---

214. Gugliotta 1997; Conley, 1999, at 786.
215. Schmickle, 1997.
216. The Reciprocal Trade Agreement Authorities Act (H.R. 2621) failed by a 180-243 vote on Sept. 25, 1998 (Democrats: 29-171; Republicans 151-71, with one independent opposed).

were facing infuriated constituents as NAFTA job losses mounted and WTO challenges against U.S. laws, which obtained front page coverage, continued. In Los Angeles, union and environmental organizations vowed to primary out nine-term incumbent Rep. Matthew Martinez (D-Calif.), an unrepentant NAFTA supporter. They succeeded in doing so – bringing fair trade leader Rep. Hilda Solis to Congress. Seven-term incumbent Tom Sawyer (D-Ohio) met a similar fate in the next election cycle, while long-term incumbent GOP Congressmen Phil English (R-Penn.) and Robin Hayes (R-N.C.) later lost their reelections over their 2005 support of the Central America Free Trade Agreement (CAFTA). These losses came as sizeable numbers of traditional GOP voters crossed party lines to support Democrats whose campaigns focused on the incumbents support for trade pacts that threatened to offshore more American jobs.

But Fast Track meant that even those members who had voted against NAFTA and the WTO were faced with the reality of trade agreements causing the very damage that they had predicted, even as they were unable to alter the trade model and avoid future damaging pacts as a result of their exclusion from the formative aspects of trade policy. As Rep. Peter DeFazio (D-Ore.) noted:

> "This is about a process that includes plausible deniability. That means there are a lot of people here who do not want to take responsibility for what is happening in America. They can say, you know, I had concerns about NAFTA. I knew there were problems with some parts of NAFTA. I knew there were problems with labor agreements, they were kind of weak, and we lost a lot of jobs there, and wages have gone down on both sides of the border. Yes, I had some real concerns about those environmental provisions. I really did not think they would clean up the border, which is one of the largest and fastest growing hazardous waste sites in the world. But I had to vote up or down, and I could not sacrifice 2 years of secret negotiations, and we will fix those things later. That is what we hear every time an agreement comes forward under Fast Track. Are Members going to blow up three years of careful secret negotiations, just because they have a minor concern about their

farmers or about the environment or about American workers? No. The herd here most times said, gee, I would have liked to do something, but I could not. Why could they not? Because they gave away that authority at the beginning. Do not give away that authority ever again.[217]"

The 1998 Fast Track debate touched both on the mechanism's overconcentration of unaccountable power in the executive branch, and its lack of a meaningful connection to trade expansion. Marcy Kaptur, who had been instrumental in attempting to beef up the 1988 Fast Track, summed up these concerns by noting on the House floor: "Fast Track is not required for good trade agreements. It is required to get bad trade deals through Congress."[218]

f. The George W. Bush Administration Kills Fast Track's Remaining Legitimacy, 2001-2008

On August 27, 2000, then-candidate George W. Bush gave a speech in Miami setting Fast Track as one of his top legislative priorities. After the election, with Republicans controlling both chambers of Congress and the White House, President Bush set out to obtain a new delegation of authority to expand the WTO and extend NAFTA-style trade agreements to additional countries, most notably through the Free Trade Agreement of the Americas (FTAA). (The FTAA was a 34-country NAFTA expansion that had been launched by Clinton shortly after NAFTA passed, but that had still not been completed when Bush took office because some of the involved countries had grown concerned about NAFTA's damaging effects in Mexico and U.S. insistence on inclusion of non-trade terms the countries could not accept.) While the Republican congressional leadership shared Bush's zeal for this agenda, public antipathy to NAFTA was high and the prospect of its expansion was unpopular in Congress, including with some members of his own party.[219]

---

217. Rep. Peter DeFazio (D-Ore.), *Congressional Record,* Sept. 25, 1998, at H8789.
218. Rep. Marcy Kaptur (D-Ohio), *Congressional Record*, Sept. 25, 1998, at H8765.
219. Destler, 2005, at 288-293.

What ensued is a long and tangled story, so here's the spoiler: passing this final delegation of Fast Track required almost two years of intense battle and major expenditure of political capital by Bush. Controversial procedural tactics included holding open the House roll call to twist arms, flip votes, and ultimately pass Fast Track by one vote in the middle of the night, just as Congress was going on recess in 2002. This victory was pyrrhic, as Bush's use of Fast Track to try to force a vote over the objections of the congressional leadership on the highly controversial Colombia FTA ultimately proved to be Fast Track's final undoing.

Indeed, Fast Track's structure provided Bush with a perfect tool to demolish what was an already shaky inter-branch relationship regarding trade-agreement negotiations and approval. Ironically, the straw that broke Fast Track's back came when Bush simply invoked the full powers that the extraordinary mechanism provided on paper that, to date, presidents had only threatened to unleash. For members of Congress, the Bush administration's use of Fast Track – to steamroll their suggestions about trade agreements' contents, implementing legislation, and vote timing – revealed exactly how the process operated, and to what degree it cut them out of a meaningful role. So as is shown in this section, not only was Congress unwilling to provide Bush with additional authority past 2007, but by 2008 even former proponents of the Fast Track process had begun discussing the need for a greatly altered system that enhanced congressional control.

But let us first share some of the key details that provide the context for the death of Fast Track. Almost immediately after entering office in 2001, the Bush administration started destroying what little remained of the so-called bipartisan "trade consensus." The Jordan FTA, which Clinton had negotiated and signed in 2000, contained somewhat improved labor provisions and for the first time contained labor provisions in its core text. The agreement passed by a wide margin under normal, non-Fast Track congressional voting procedures in the first year of the Bush administration. When Democrats who had traditionally opposed FTAs announced their support for the Jordan pact – even though it contained other provisions which they opposed, limiting access to generic medicines – they stated that the improved labor standards were but the *first step* toward a more comprehensive overhaul of the U.S. FTA model. The Bush administration's response was to invalidate the FTA's labor provisions by writing to the King of Jordan and declaring it would not enforce them.[220]

In the summer of 2001, the Bush administration launched a campaign for what it called a "clean Fast Track," i.e. one that did not address the reservoir of bipartisan concerns about Congress' ever-shrinking authority under past delegations or the agreements they had produced. These included GOP concerns about the pacts' submission of the United States to the authority of extra-judicial World Bank and UN tribunals, and Democratic concerns about the lack of enforceable labor, environmental and other standards.[221] In the effort to sideline such concerns, Ways & Means Chair Bill Thomas (R-Calif.) played a key role. Thomas' abrasive personal style and open contempt for committee Democrats resulted in a bill that infuriated many members who in the past had supported Fast Track delegations.[222] Thomas' bill contained substantially weaker language on labor standards than those in the 1988 Fast Track.[223] Indeed, his proposed legislation included language designed to deny Fast Track treatment to trade bills containing the Jordan-style labor provisions. This language stated that Fast Track procedures would only apply to labor and environmental provisions that are "directly related to trade," "consistent with the sovereignty of the U.S.," and do "not affect a country's ability to make changes to its laws that are consistent with sound macroeconomic development."[224]

As early as June 2001, House Democrats – from Minority Leader Gephardt (who had supported the 1991 and 1993 Fast Track extensions) to the pro-"free trade" New Democrats – were united against the Thomas bill and Bush's overall approach. This tactical unity

---

220. Bolle, 2003. (On the thinking of congressional Democrats, see Bolle's excerpt of the floor statement of Rep. Sherrod Brown (D-Ohio)).
221. IUT, 2001a; IUT, 2001b.
222. Destler, 2005, at 290-291.
223. Pier, 2006, at 85.
224. Section 3(b)(3).

was driven by a range of calculations. In one corner were Democrats inclined to support free trade, but concerned about Fast Track's undermining of the separation of powers, thus enabling more over-reaching NAFTA and WTO-style agreements that invaded Congress' domestic policymaking prerogatives. In another were members that assumed the Bush administration would eventually cede to their demands for political cover in the form of enhanced labor standards (enforceable or not), as had past administrations. In still another were Representatives that used the labor-rights issue as proxy for wider critiques about Fast Track and the agreements it had enabled. Given the mood in Congress on trade, even one of the most pro-Fast Track, pro-NAFTA Democrats in Congress, Rep. Jim Moran (D-Va.), announced, "a clean bill is a dead bill."[225]

The administration tried several approaches to overcome this opposition. First, they invoked arguments about the alleged economic success of past Fast Tracked deals like NAFTA. Thanks to record NAFTA trade deficits and soaring U.S. manufacturing job loss, however, this line of argumentation did not gain traction in Congress. Later, after the 9-11 attacks, the administration shifted its messaging to a national-security frame. Bush's U.S. Trade Representative Robert Zoellick, for instance, wrote a *Washington Post* editorial entitled "Countering Terror with Trade," which argued that Congress needed to pass Fast Track to show "Today's enemies... that the United States is committed to global leadership." This security-mongering argument has been a common ploy ever since.[226]

In this instance, a central argument aimed at corralling GOP support for Fast Track was that Republican members of Congress had to demonstrate to the world their support of the president. With this appeal, GOP congressional leaders began to move the bill.[227]

By October 2001, Ways & Means Committee ranking member Charles Rangel (D-N.Y.) and committee trade leaders Levin and Robert Matsui (D-Calif.) developed an alternative Fast Track proposal that would have improved labor, environmental and other ne-

225. IUT, 2001b; IUT, 2001c; IUT, 2001d.
226. Gates and Santos, 2008.
227. Blustein, 2001.

gotiating objectives. The proposal also addressed some criticisms of NAFTA-style rules granting foreign investors special privileges, by including language requiring that under U.S. trade agreements, the mere diminution in the value of an investment by a domestic policy would not constitute a compensable expropriation. It also called for establishment of a "non-political screening process for investor-state claims."[228]

The proposal offered members of Congress more opportunities to initiate Fast Track disapproval resolutions, although it did not alter the basic structure of Fast Track. Their bill also sought to impose more accountability over executive-branch negotiators in regards to Congress' negotiating objectives, although it repeated the Gephardt-Richardson proposal's problematic designation of the president as certifier that Congress' objectives had been met. The bill did do so in a manner that unfortunately would have transferred away congressional authority to yet another set of actors – the private sector advisors who mainly represented various business interests. Ninety days before signing a trade agreement, the president would be required to certify to Congress that the principal negotiating objectives had been met. At that point, not the Congress, but the industry representatives in advisory groups would have 30 days to vote to second this assessment. If a majority of the advisory committees disagreed, Fast Track procedures would not apply to the agreement.[229]

Whatever the merits of having business representatives review the portions of the agreement related to their industry, the construct still meant that Congress was not in the position of reviewing the entire contents of the agreement to determine if on balance it served the national interest and preserved the key tenets of U.S. governance with respect to safeguarding U.S. sovereignty, federalism and checks and balances.

Rangel and his colleagues offered this proposal as a "motion to recommit" during the debate on the bill on December 6, 2001. (This legislative procedure allows members critical of a bill to call for a vote on whether to send it back to committee with specific amendment

228. IUT, 2001e. For greater detail on the investor-state mechanism, see Bottari and Wallach, 2005.
229. Text of the proposal is available at *Congressional Record,* 147, Dec. 6, 2001, at H9030. Section 7(b) describes the new trade advisory proposal.

instructions.) But the motion failed, and the final passage vote on the Thomas bill was called. When time for the vote had elapsed and the large vote-board looming over the House floor showed a majority against Fast Track, frustrated congressmembers yelled from the floor that time had expired – and Fast Track had been defeated.[230]

But that was not to be. In the aisles of the House chamber, the House Republican leadership rounded up several Republicans from textile districts simultaneously berating them and offering them special deals, including a promise to pass legislation amending several U.S. trade-preference programs in order to win their support. Three Republican Fast Track critics then changed their stance thanks to this last minute maneuver, including Rep. Robin Hayes (R-N.C.), who cast the deciding vote.[231] Hastert slammed down the gavel the second the "yes" vote number bested the "no" vote tally. The House thus passed the Thomas bill by the narrowest of margins (215 to 214), after Speaker Dennis Hastert stretched House rules to keep voting open for twenty minutes after the official clock had tolled.

Many of the same issues that marked the House debate transferred over to the Senate fight. Thomas' 2001 Fast Track, in addition to rolling back labor-standards language (even the strongest version of which had proven ineffective in promoting improved labor conditions in trade partner countries in the past), gave enormous discretion for negotiators to extend extremely problematic FTA investor-rights provisions that submitted the United States to extrajudicial foreign tribunals. This latter issue became a prominent focus of the Senate debate on the Finance Committee's Fast Track bill. Thanks to various shuffles in Senate leadership, the Senate bill was more moderate than Thomas'. Republicans and Democrats had twice exchanged the Finance Committee's chairmanship during 2001-02 (from William Roth (R-Del.) to Max Baucus (D-Mont.) to Charles Grassley (R-Iowa).) Unlike the House side, however, where the Democratic gatekeeper-

---

230. Nelson, 2001.
231. Specifically, this deal would require that imports of knit and woven fabrics from various preference-program countries be dyed, finished and printed in the United States to receive duty-free treatment. As a result, Rep. Jim DeMint (R-S.C.) switched his vote from "nay" to "aye," and Reps. Cass Ballenger (R-N.C.) and Robin Hayes (R-N.C.) lodged their "aye" votes after he did. See IUT, 2001g.

committee leaders put forward ideas (squashed by Thomas) to reform modestly the structure of Fast Track, Baucus supported a bill largely drafted by his Republican counterparts in exchange for White House commitments on expanding the trade adjustment assistance provided for workers who lost jobs to trade agreements.

The 2002 Senate Fast Track debate featured an unprecedented month-long floor fight, from April 25 to May 23. While final Senate passage was expected – traditionally the Senate has passed trade bills by wide margins – the extended debate and wide array of amendments to the Finance proposal was unusual. Sen. John Kerry (D-Mass.) offered an amendment on the foreign investor rights/foreign tribunals rules that was a stronger version of the Rangel-Levin-Matsui proposal. The Kerry amendment included a requirement significantly narrowing what types of U.S. laws could be brought before foreign tribunals for review. The White House campaigned ferociously against the amendment, which was defeated with help from Baucus. The White House similarly attacked and defeated a modest amendment by Sen. Joseph Lieberman of Connecticut that would have rolled back some of the new anti-labor and anti-environmental standards language.[232]

Meanwhile, a bipartisan team of senators, Mark Dayton (D-Minn.) and Larry Craig (R-Idaho), offered an amendment forbidding U.S. negotiators from rolling back U.S. anti-dumping laws in future trade agreements. Unlike the Kerry amendment, this proposal was structured so that it would create a *binding* congressional mandate upon which Fast Track would be conditioned. Dayton-Craig called for the waiver of Fast Track rules with respect to provisions of a trade agreement that undermined existing U.S. anti-dumping or countervailing duty laws. It did so in a manner that empowered the Senate to determine if the negotiating objective had been met, albeit only after the agreement had already been signed. The amendment empowered any Senator to raise a point of order calling for Fast Track procedures to be terminated with respect to the provisions that undermined existing U.S. trade law. In effect, the amendment restored normal Senate vote procedures for such provisions, meaning amendments would be permitted and the

---

232. IUT, 2002b.

Senate could reject that aspect of the agreement while consideration of the rest of the agreement would proceed under Fast Track rules. The Dayton-Craig amendment was supported in the Senate on May 14, 2002 by a strong bipartisan vote of 61-38.[233] The Senate passed the overall Fast Track package – as an amendment to a bill on Andean trade preferences – on May 23 on a 66-30 vote.

The House and Senate had passed different Fast Track bills, with some Senate provisions (such as on TAA) having never received a House vote. The two chambers needed to convene a conference to prepare the bills for final passage. Thomas' procedural stunts, however, were far from over. On June 26, the Ways & Means chair and his allies on the House Rules Committee proposed a so-called "self-executing rule" that, in addition to the standard procedure of requesting a conference, took the unprecedented step of simultaneously approving vast portions of the Senate bill that the House had never voted on. The measure also stripped the Dayton-Craig amendment. Democrats questioned its constitutionality. In the words of Rep. Alcee Hastings (D-Fla.): "Last week, [Thomas] accused the other body of all sorts of underhanded legislative witchcraft. And how do we answer that in the House? With our own Harry Potter-like sorcery."[234] Rep. Nancy Pelosi (D-Calif.) added, "This is a very dark day for the House of Representatives."[235] The "rule" passed by a 216-215 vote, with 94 percent of Democrats opposed.[236]

After a month in conference, the bill came to the House floor for final passage in the middle of the night on July 27. This latest version added a remarkable provision, dubbed the Gramm amendment. This was a massive loophole to the bill's (already weak) labor and environmental standards. It stated that a country could explicitly get out of the requirement to enforce its own labor and environmental law (not just implicitly by repeatedly failing to "strive" to do so) if its government decided to spend its labor enforcement dollars on other priorities.[237]

---

233. IUT, 2002a.
234. Rep. Alcee Hastings (D-Fla.), *Congressional Record,* 148, June 26, 2002, at H3953.
235. Rep. Nancy Pelosi (D-Calif.), *Congressional Record,* 148, June 26, 2002, at H3961.
236. H. Res. 450, "Relating to consideration of the Senate amendment to the bill (H.R. 3009) to extend the Andean Trade Preference Act, to grant additional trade benefits under that Act, and for other purposes," approved June 26, 2002.
237. Public Law 107-210, § 2102 (11).

In the words of Rep. David Wu (D-Ore.): "To deem this a loophole is to call the hole in the side of the Titanic a small leak."[238] The final bill also gutted the Senate-passed Dayton-Craig amendment, including instead hortatory and unenforceable language on dumping. Additionally, the final version gutted much of Baucus' TAA proposal.[239]

Despite only 25 out of 210 House Democrats supporting the bill and 27 House Republicans opposing, the Orwellian-named Bipartisan Trade Promotion Authority Act of 2002 passed the House by a 215-212 vote at 3 a.m. the morning after Congress' summer recess was to have started.[240] The approval again came after the vote clock was stopped. Levin summed up the view of many when he said that the mechanism "maintains a minimal, meaningless, and last-minute role for Congress, at a time when trade policy is increasingly intertwined with all areas of domestic policy."[241] Perhaps the most poignant commentary came from Robert Matsui, one of the House's leading Democratic advocates of NAFTA and the WTO. He urged his colleagues to vote down Fast Track, saying:

> "I stand here before you today as a free trader… But this vote is about much more than that. It's about the fact that the very nature of international trade has changed radically. Trade is no longer primarily about tariffs and quotas. It's about changing domestic laws. The constitutional authority to make law is at the heart of our role as a Congress and of our sovereignty as a nation. When international trade negotiators sit down to hammer out agreements, they are talking about harmonizing 'non-tariff barriers to trade' that may include everything from antitrust laws to food safety.
>
> Now, I believe the President and the USTR should be able to negotiate trade deals as efficiently as possible. There's no

---

238. Rep. David Wu (D-Ore.), *Congressional Record,* 148, July 27, 2002, at H5974.
239. IUT, 2002c.
240. The House passed an initial version of Fast Track (H.R. 3005) by a 215-214 vote on Dec. 6, 2001 (D: 21-189; R: 194-23, with 2 independents opposed). The Senate passed an amended version attached to trade preferences legislation (H.R. 3009) on May 23, 2002 by a 66-30 vote (D: 25-25; R: 40-5, with one independent in favor). The conference version passed the House on July 27 by a 215-212 vote (D: 25-183; R: 190-27, with 2 independents opposed), and the Senate on August 1 on a 64-32 vote (D: 20-29; R: 43-5, with one independent in favor).
241. Stokes, 2002.

question about that. But that does not mean that Congress must concede to the Executive Branch its constitutional authority over foreign commerce and domestic law without adequate assurances that Congress will be an active participant in the process. Congress should be a partner, not a mere spectator or occasional consultant to the process. The Thomas bill does not ensure that. Think about what may be bargained away at the negotiating table: our own domestic environmental protections ... food safety laws ... competition policies. That's the air we breathe, the food our children eat, and the way Americans do business...

The nature of trade has changed, and Fast Track authority must change with it. I ardently believe in the principles of free trade. But I will not put my constitutional authority over domestic law and my responsibility to my own constituents on a fast track to the executive branch. I urge my colleagues to vote no on this legislation."[242]

Overall, the Bush administration used Fast Track much more aggressively than previous presidents, passing eight NAFTA-style trade deals, including CAFTA (which passed the House by a two-vote margin in 2005 in the middle of the night, largely along party lines). In that instance, the bill passed once again after the vote clock was stopped and Hayes had been persuaded to reverse his "no" vote.[243] (Hayes lost re-election in 2008 to Larry Kissell, a social-studies teacher who had been moved to run for Congress because of Hayes' repeated trade vote flip-flops, and whose campaign focused primarily on the damage these votes had caused his district.) Notably, Bush was not successful in expanding the WTO or establishing the FTAA, which had been the original justifications for asking for Fast Track.

The Bush administration's strong-arming of the legislative branch via Fast Track was educational for many members of Congress who had not previously realized the full details and implications of the delegation authority. These lessons were delivered through a series of

---

242. Rep. Robert Matsui (D-Calif.), *Congressional Record*, 147, Dec. 6, 2001, at H9025.
243. See Tucker, 2006a, at 23.

incidents and actions. First, Bush dispensed with some of the friendly if largely meaningless courtesies presidents had provided to the trade gatekeeper committees, which had provided a patina of legislative-executive branch cooperation.

For instance, in 2006, after a front-page *New York Times* exposé detailed the prevalence of horrific sweatshop conditions in Jordanian factories producing for the U.S. market under the Jordan FTA, Sen. Kent Conrad (D-N.D.) offered an amendment to the Oman FTA in the Senate Finance Committee's "mock markup" session. Conrad's amendment would have prohibited goods made with slave labor from entering the United States. He noted that he offered the amendment, which was approved by the committee on a bipartisan, unanimous 18-0 vote, because FTA partner countries had promised Congress in the past to make certain changes to their laws but then failed to do so after the vote.[244] Not only did the Bush administration refuse to add this amendment to the Oman FTA's implementing legislation, but it argued moreover that it was *prohibited* by Fast Track from amending the FTA. Conrad subsequently told the press that he had "really lost confidence in this process... I won't subject American workers to that kind of competition."[245]

Next, the arbitrariness of the authority provided to the executive branch under Fast Track delegation was further highlighted – in this case to the ire of some Republican congresspeople – when the Bush administration proceeded to do the very thing it claimed it could not on previous trade deals: post-signing alterations of FTA text signed under Fast Track. This led, for instance, to two Republican Finance Committee members, Sens. Orrin Hatch (R-Utah) and Jon Kyl (R-Ariz.), voting against the Peru FTA during a September 21 mock-mark up of the bill, citing the *post-facto* changes to the FTA's terms.[246]

The post-signing changes to the Peru FTA came in the context of a May 10, 2007 Bush administration announcement that its FTAs with Peru, Colombia, Panama, and South Korea would include certain labor, environmental and drug-patent provision improvements that Rangel and Levin – now back in the majority with the 2006 Democratic sweep

---

244. He referred to Bahrain's promise in advance of an FTA vote with that country to dismantle its boycott of Israel, which it did not. See IUT, 2006a.
245. Blinkhorn, 2006.
246. Vaughan, 2007.

– had sought. While the changes were viewed by many Democratic members and constituency groups as good first steps towards improving the U.S. trade agreement model, they infuriated many Republicans and created ample political and procedural problems.

Republicans that had supported the Gramm amendment's tight Fast Track strictures on inclusion of labor standards stood by in disbelief as the most robust labor standards ever included in a U.S. trade agreement were added to the four agreements, this despite the pacts having been signed and sealed. In addition, new environmental terms were added *post facto*. Under Fast Track rules, the revised agreements would come to a vote without opportunities for amendments.

Meanwhile, the deal to modify the agreements had been negotiated without input of most Democratic House members with regard to what changes they considered essential. Many members of the Democratic House Caucus were furious when the deal was announced as a *New Trade Policy for America*, even though it did not address their priority concerns. The final deal was unveiled in a surprise news conference in the Capitol featuring administration representatives and Democratic and Republican congressional leaders who announced plans to move forward with at least two of Bush's free trade agreements revised to include the new labor and other provisions, even as some Democratic congressional opponents of that plan gathered in the rear of the room fuming and Republican Senators Hatch and Kyl announced their opposition.[247]

Statements about Fast Track that Rangel and Baucus had made, after being elevated to chairs of their committees in 2007, compounded the anger of congressional Democrats. The chairs suggested that they would be inclined to provide President Bush with *new* Fast Track authority.[248] Much of the new House majority Democratic leadership and caucus members were focused on investigating and countering what they deemed abuse by President Bush of his *existing* authorities and broad disdain for Congress' constitutional role. Thus, in a replay of congressional sentiment with respect to Clinton's 1997 Fast Track request, for Democrats the notion of granting Bush any additional discretion or authority was not popular.

247. Abrams, 2007; AP, 2007.
248. McGrane, 2007.

The uproar from many Democratic House members and base groups about the May 10 deal colored the ongoing discussions among congressional Democrats regarding the next steps on trade policy. In June 2007, the Democratic House leadership issued a written statement stating that they would not support further Fast Track for President Bush.[249] The document, signed by Speaker Pelosi, Majority Leader Steny Hoyer (D-Md.), Rangel and Levin, demonstrated unity against further Fast Track for Bush. It also signaled that Rangel's early 2007 statements on Fast Track did not represent the position of the united House leadership.[250]

And these were just the domestic problems – there was also the matter of getting the trading partners to accept these last minute changes. The Peru deal had already been signed on April 12, 2006, and the Colombia deal on November 22, 2006. And Bush's authority to negotiate trade agreements under Fast Track expired at midnight on Saturday, June 30, 2007. This left only 50 days to renegotiate the already-signed Peru and Colombia deals, and finalize the deals with Panama and Korea. The administration made this deadline with only hours to spare. A reworked deal with Peru was signed at 10 a.m. on June 25, 2007, and approved by the Peruvian legislature two days later. The deals with Colombia and Panama followed on June 28. The Korea deal was only inked on June 30 – just hours before Fast Track expired.

The Peru FTA passed in November 2007, but with a majority of Democrats – including 12 of 19 House committee chairs – voting against it.[251] (And, as if to top it all off, in January 2009 Bush implemented the FTA as one of his final acts in office, without Peru having complied with the labor and environmental improvements that Rangel and Levin had won in the FTA text.)

Yet the Fast Track structure might have survived President Bush were it not for one, final and insulting Fast Track move. In perhaps the

249. Pelosi, 2007.
250. Hennig, 2007; Swanson, 2007.
251. Strawbridge, 2007.

most stunning of all of Bush's maneuvers, the president broke traditional Fast Track etiquette by submitting the Colombia FTA for a
vote, over the explicit *opposition* of the House leadership and without
the courtesy of going through the mock mark-up process. The trade
deal was highly controversial to begin with, since many in and out of
Congress considered Colombia to have such severe labor and human
rights problems (and its then-president to be so entangled with righ-
twing paramilitaries) that the country should not have been considered
for an FTA.[252]

The president's right to force a vote in this manner had of course always been a key aspect of Fast Track. But past presidents had avoided
formally exercising it, perhaps to avoid highlighting to all in Congress
that, under Fast Track, the president could seize control of the legislative branch's floor schedule. Corporate supporters of the Colombia
FTA had urged the White House not to use what they dubbed the "nu-
clear option," for fear of what such an encroachment of power would
do to the future of the Fast Track process.[253] Disregarding this counsel, the administration dispensed altogether with the "mock mark ups,"
submitting legislation it had written without even informal congressional review and triggering Fast Track's 60-day forced-vote clock in
the House.

Bush's tactic proved to be the death knell for Fast Track. Speaker Pelosi
and the House Rules Committee responded to Bush's unprecedented
action by reasserting Congress' constitutional prerogatives. The Rules
Committee formulated a new rule for the Colombia FTA, which
removed the mandatory 60-day vote timeline, and the House passed
this new rule on April 10, 2008.[254] In Pelosi's words, "We are the
people's House. Their timetable should be our timetable."[255]

The damage that Bush's move had wrought was signaled by the comments of previously uncritical supporters of Fast Track. Rep. Ike Skelton (D-Mo.), who had systematically supported past Fast Tracks and

252. Sweeney, 2008; Nichols, 2008.
253. IUT, 2008; Homan, 2008.
254. H. Res. 1092, passed April 10, 2008, by a 224-195 margin (Democrats: 218-10; Republicans:
6-185). For a behind the scenes look at the rules change, see O'Connor and Kady, 2008.
255. Speaker Nancy Pelosi (D-Calif.), *Congressional Record,* 154, April 10, 2008, at H2182.

"trade" agreements, noted: "Article I, Section 8 of the U.S. Constitution grants Congress the power to regulate commerce with foreign nations … On April 8, 2008, the Administration took the unprecedented step of delivering the Colombia Trade Promotion Agreement to Congress without having fully consulted with the House and the Senate. In my view, the Administration's maneuver seriously jeopardizes prospects for the trade agreement's passage in the House."[256] Sen. Richard Lugar (R-Ind.) issued a statement: "I support the U.S.-Colombia Trade Promotion Agreement … However, I am concerned by the politically inhospitable circumstances in which the agreement is being sent to the U.S. Congress. The Colombian free-trade agreement faces stiff opposition because many in Congress believe the Colombian government has not taken sufficient measures to ensure the safety and security of its workers. This opposition could derail its passage this year."[257] Rep. Gregory Meeks (D-N.Y.), one of the few Democratic supporters of CAFTA and a fierce supporter of the Colombia FTA, commented: "I'm disappointed… You don't take these kinds of agreements up unless you have an agreement. I think this hurts it."[258]

One long-time trade expert, Fred Bergsten, denounced the Colombia FTA Fast Track meltdown as "the gravest threat to the global trading system in decades."[259] The *Financial Times* noted that "Even before this week, Fast Track has had a rocky history and has sometimes been suspended, for example during the latter years of the Clinton administration following the passage of the North American Free Trade Agreement."[260]

America's fifth trade regime, Fast Track, had also coincided with a return to Robber Baron-era low rates of U.S. per capita income growth. From 1973 to 2008, the average annual real per capita growth rate was only 2 percent – below that of America's first 100 years, and that of its post-war Golden Age.[261]

---

256. Rep. Ike Skelton (D-Mo.), *Congressional Record,* 154, April 10, 2008, at H2187.
257. Lugar, 2008.
258. O'Connor and McGrane, 2008.
259. Bergsten, 2008.
260. Politi, 2008.
261. For more on the outcomes of Fast-Track enabled trade pacts, see Public Citizen, 2013 ("Prosperity Undermined During Era of Fast Tracked NAFTA and WTO Model Trade Agreements.")

g. Zombie Fast Track years, 2009-12

Although the Fifth Regime was officially over, Bush's completion of negotiations on the Korea and Panama agreements before the June 2007 expiration meant that these deals would still enjoy Fast Track protection if and when a future president chose to introduce implementing legislation for them to Congress. To paraphrase Nixon's advisor John Connally, this meant they would stick around like a loaded shotgun – waiting to be unleashed by some future president.

Bush's aggressive use of Fast Track made it politically impossible for many in Washington to advocate for such a move. Criticism of Fast Tracked trade policy was electorally potent in the 2006 and 2008 national elections, as increasing scores of Democratic and Republican candidates alike took out paid ads to criticize status quo trade policy and the U.S. job offshoring it had fueled.[262] This issue figured prominently in the 2007-08 presidential primaries, with all eight Democratic candidates and some Republican candidates pledging changes to trade policy. Candidate Barack Obama promised to "replace Fast Track with a process that includes criteria determining appropriate negotiating partners ... I will ensure that Congress plays a strong and informed role in our international economic policy and in any future agreements we pursue and in our efforts to amend existing agreements."[263]

Following the 2008 election, there were some early good indications that Obama would keep his campaign promises to reform the U.S. trade agreement model and the process used to negotiate, sign and approve agreements. Obama's reported first pick for USTR – Rep. Xavier Becerra (D-Calif.) – voted against Fast Track on three out of three occasions. In the 2001 floor debate on Fast Track, Becerra pointed out that the procedure was completely unnecessary, as "Over the past 250 years of our Nation's existence, for only 20 of those years, from 1974 to 1994, has this body granted the President authority for fast tracking any trade agreement. In those 20 years, five agreements were

262. Tucker, 2006b; Slevin and Tucker, 2007; Tucker, 2008.
263. IFTC, 2007.

signed. In contrast, during the 8 years of the Clinton administration, 300 agreements were signed with countries from Belarus to Japan to Uzbekistan. We can do this without Fast Track."

Obama eventually settled on former Dallas Mayor Ron Kirk as his USTR pick. While Kirk was not well known in trade circles, there were also some positive signs in his appointment. According to the *Dallas Morning News* (3/8/02), Kirk had blasted his Democratic primary opponent Ken Bentsen in the 2002 U.S. Senate race for his Fast Track vote, saying he cast "the decisive vote to give this trade bill a one-vote victory in the House of Representatives without any real guarantee of help for workers who lose their jobs because of trade."

On February 27, 2009, USTR released "The President's Trade Policy Agenda," which stated that the administration "will use all available tools to address this economic crisis including achieving access to new markets for American businesses large and small. One of these tools is the authority Congress can grant the Executive to negotiate trade agreements and bring them to the legislature for an up or down vote. We will only ask for renewed trade negotiating authority after engaging in extensive consultation with Congress to establish the proper constraints on that authority and after we have assessed our priorities and made clear to this body and the American people what we intend to do with it."

Any mention of seeking a new grant of trade authority received considerable push-back. [264] Especially in light of the urgent demands of the economic crisis and reminders of how Clinton's early prioritization of unpopular trade initiatives had sapped his political capital for passing health care reform, the administration shelved plans to advance the three leftover Bush FTAs or seek Fast Track. In December 2009, Kirk again floated the idea of requesting Fast Track,[265] an idea that again went nowhere. On June 26, 2010, Obama announced intentions to move forward with the Korea FTA.[266] But again, little happened. However, then within weeks of the 2010 elections, Obama announced

---

264. IUT, 2009b.
265. IUT, 2009c.
266. IUT, 2010a.

some alterations to auto tariff phase-in schedules and other alterations to the Korea FTA's auto-related provisions that would give him some political cover to move the deal forward. By mid-2011, side deals on labor and tax haven abuses were hammered out with Colombia and Panama respectively.[267] Calls by leading Democratic Ways & Means members to connect compliance with the labor side agreement to the Colombia FTA's actual implementation were rejected by the administration. Whatever one's views of the Korea FTA alterations or Colombia and Panama side deals – and reactions were decidedly mixed – the move towards votes on the pacts created interesting challenges with respect to Fast Track rules.

Fast Track was long expired, and its special congressional floor consideration rules only applied on the basis of Congress having been given notice *before* the agreements were signed and entered into. USTR maintained that the changes to the Korea deal represented a separate agreement and thus did not undermine the notice requirements of Fast Track.[268] Yet, in fact the new arrangements explicitly altered tariff phase-out schedules set in the underlying FTA. The only way Congress could have challenged that arbitrary claim would have been to have a majority act to change the default Fast Track floor rules. The Colombia and Panama side deals clearly did not alter the underlying agreements. Indeed, their lack of connection to the pacts was the basis for much criticism about the side deals' ineffectiveness.

Meanwhile, the status of Fast Track floor procedures for the Colombia FTA, which Bush had previously submitted to Congress, drew split opinions from the House and Senate parliamentarians. Most trade experts understood that once a president had submitted an agreement under Fast Track, that agreement's opportunity to be considered under Fast Track extraordinary floor rules was "used up." When asked for an opinion on the matter, the House parliamentarian agreed that Fast Track rules no longer applied to the Colombia FTA. However, the Senate parliamentarian ruled that the special procedures did apply and normal Senate rules would be suspended in the event of

267. Tucker, 2011.
268. IUT, 2011a.

115

Colombia FTA consideration, providing yet a further expansion of Fast Track's executive branch powers. While Fast Track floor rules were automatically applied to all three deals in the Senate, House Republicans wrote a special rule explicitly applying the Fast Track floor procedures to each of the deals.

Congress passed all three deals on October 12, although over two-thirds of Democrats voted against them, and against their own president. Indeed, the Colombia and Korea FTAs obtained the highest percentages of Democratic no votes relative to any past trade votes under Democratic presidents. [269]

President Obama seemed to recognize the politically problematic nature of this "accomplishment" and hastily cancelled the Rose Garden signing ceremony for the three deals.[270] But just weeks later, as the 2012 election drew ever closer and public opinion polls showed transpartisan opposition to the recently-passed FTAs,[271] Obama's USTR appeared to have not gotten the political memo and was again floating the idea that "we are going to have to have" Fast Track for a new Trans-Pacific trade deal.[272]

USTR Kirk was referring to the Trans-Pacific Partnership free trade agreement. Despite having no delegation of trade authority, much less congressional consent to prioritize negotiations with the involved countries, the Bush II administration had joined negotiations on what would become the TPP in 2008 with Brunei, Chile, New Zealand and Singapore.[273] President Bush's USTR sent a second TPP notice to Congress in December 2008 expanding the list of partners involved in the Trans-Pacific FTA to include Australia, Vietnam and Peru.[274] Shortly after President Obama's inauguration, USTR published in the January 26, 2009 Federal Register a "Notice of intent to initiate negotiations on a Trans-Pacific Partnership (TPP) free trade agreement with Singapore, Chile, New Zealand, Brunei Darussalam, Australia, Peru and Vietnam,

---

269. Tucker and Wallach, 2011.
270. Runningen, 2011.
271. National Journal, 2011.
272. IUT, 2011c.
273. Schwab, 2008a.
274. Schwab, 2008b.

request for comments, and notice of public hearing."[275]

Since candidate Obama had pledged to reform the U.S. trade agreement model and work with Congress to establish a new trade authority mechanism that provided Congress a more robust role, the notion that TPP negotiations would continue as if an election had not occurred generated considerable pushback by some in Congress and among Democratic constituencies. On February 24, the Obama administration asked the TPP countries to delay negotiations that had been scheduled for March 2009 so that the new administration could appoint trade officials and review its trade policy.[276] A formal review never occurred.

The manner in which the Obama administration proceeded to handle the TPP process, which as of the writing of this book has included 16 rounds of negotiations, only served to exacerbate congressional concerns that Congress was once again being cut out of U.S. trade agreement policymaking. To start with, congressional and private sector consultations about *whether* to participate in TPP negotiations were perceived by participants as perfunctory, even meaningless. The sense that executive branch officials were merely going through the motions of taking input rather than listening to Congress was repeatedly reinforced.

For instance, as consultations began, following a May 18 speech at the U.S. Chamber of Commerce, recently-confirmed USTR Ron Kirk told reporters that the Obama administration *would* pursue a TPP agreement.[277] USTR then issued a clarification that no formal decision had been made on whether the United States would continue with TPP talks. But Kirk's own words before the gathering of business supporters of the TPP painted a revealing picture about the administration's top trade official's perspective on the "consultations":

> "I couldn't think of a better, more welcoming environment than being right here at the Chamber.... But considering some of the audiences that I've been in over the last 60 days, I needed a little bit of home cooking, so to speak. So I feel like I'm very much

---

275. USTR, 2009b.
276. IUT, 2009a.
277. IUT, 2009d.

preaching to the choir, and if so, please don't be offended... In a time when there are, frankly, a lot of our colleagues, a lot of our friends, that are skeptical about trade – whether there ought to be any next steps at all, it's great to be with an audience that is as eager as we are at USTR to map a new course for the future...

...And God forbid, I sure am not going to try to predict what's going to happen at the Congress. I mean, there's – I'm among friends. We are in – trade is a really tough sell among some of my friends in Congress when our economy's going well. Trade's a really tough sell in this environment..."[278]

The superficiality of the consultation process was perhaps most clearly illustrated when Congress was taken by surprise by the ultimate announcement that the Obama administration would continue with the TPP negotiations. Immediately before a presidential trip to Asia in November of 2009, GOP and Democratic congressional trade leaders were briefed by USTR that consultations would continue and no TPP announcement was forthcoming. However, days later on November 13, 2009, President Obama announced at an event in Tokyo that the United States would "engage" with the Trans-Pacific Partnership.[279]

On December 14, 2009, USTR Kirk formally notified Congress "that the President intends to enter into negotiation of a regional, Asia-Pacific trade agreement, known as the Trans-Pacific Partnership (TPP) Agreement, with the objective of shaping a high-standard, broad-based regional agreement."[280] The House caucus explicitly focused on trade had still not been consulted. They sent a letter to Kirk requesting a meeting and calling for a serious review of the U.S. trade agreement model before engaging in any negotiations.[281]

Congress' interest was well justified. The pact has 29 chapters, only five of which deal with traditional trade matters. The rest of the TPP negotiations delve deeply into matters under the jurisdiction of Congress and state legislatures. As with the WTO and NAFTA, U.S. domestic policy would be required to conform to these expansive

278. Kirk, 2009a.
279. USTR, 2009a.
280. Kirk, 2009b.
281. HTWG, 2010.

non-trade rules. And, unlike domestic legislation, changes to these rules would only be possible if all of the involved countries agreed. If completed, the TPP would not only be the largest U.S. "trade" agreement since the WTO, but perhaps the last one that the United States negotiates. TPP is being designed as a docking agreement which, if completed, would be open to be joined by any country willing to meet its terms. But despite TPP's enormous potential impact and scope, Congress' role has been more limited than on any past U.S. trade agreement. And the negotiations have been conducted under conditions of unprecedented secrecy.

While the 34 nations involved in FTAA negotiations agreed to release a full draft text of that pact in 2001, the Obama administration has explicitly refused to do so for TPP, even after announcing an October 2013 deadline to sign the deal. In contrast, even the WTO, hardly a paradigm of transparency, posts key negotiating texts on its website.

Perhaps most shocking, the administration has denied access to most members of Congress to review even the U.S. negotiating proposals for the TPP. This stands in stark contrast to past practice, when any member of Congress was able to review such documents and indeed the draft texts of an agreement itself in secure readings rooms in the U.S. Capitol, as were congressional staff with appropriate security clearances. While administration officials have conducted briefings for congressional staff about the TPP and responded to requests to meet with members of Congress to discuss it, Congress has been denied the most basic information even about what the executive branch is proposing – ostensibly on behalf of Congress, given that Congress' constitutional role is to set U.S. trade policy and the executive branch's role is to conduct negotiations to achieve Congress' goals.

In addition, members of Congress have been denied observer status at TPP negotiating rounds. This stands in contrast to NAFTA and WTO negotiations, when interested members of Congress were made part of official U.S. negotiating delegations and trade negotiators provided real-time briefings and consulted regularly with the members during each day's negotiations. But with respect to the TPP, the administration has explicitly rejected repeated requests by Republican and Democratic members alike to participate as observers.[282] The unprecedented exclusion of Congress has generated anger from improbable quarters, including Rep. Darrell Issa (R-Calif.), the Chairman of the House Oversight Committee and a longtime supporter of "free trade" agreements:

> "The U.S. Trade Representative has once again chosen to block Congress from observing negotiations for this vital trade agreement over which the House and Senate have fundamental constitutional responsibility.
>
> The TPP process should be transparent and open to oversight, not a secretive backroom negotiation. TPP agreements impact multiple sectors of the American economy--especially our ability to innovate and create new intellectual property, as well as preserve an open Internet.
>
> Congress has a constitutional duty to oversee trade negotiations and not simply act as a rubber stamp to deals about which they were kept in the dark. While I had hoped the TPP would permit me to observe this round of the negotiation process firsthand, our efforts to open TPP negotiations up to transparency will continue."[283]

Even Sen. Ron Wyden (D-Ore.), the chairman of the Senate Finance Trade Subcommittee, which has formal jurisdiction over the pact, was denied access to the draft TPP text. His security-cleared staff was denied access to even the U.S. proposals to the negotiations. This led Wyden, a strong supporter of NAFTA, the WTO and past U.S. trade pacts to resort to submitting legislation in 2012 requiring that the administration provide such access. The degree to which Congress' constitutional role over trade policy had been eroded during the TPP process was highlighted by the bill's name - the Congressional Oversight Over Trade Negotiations Act. Wyden's Senate floor statement[284]

---

282. See, for example, IUT 2012a and IUT 2012b.
283. Issa, 2012.
284. Sen. Ron Wyden (D-Ore.), *Congressional Record*, 158, May 23, 2012, at S3517.

upon introducing the bill, S 3225, described the sorry state of affairs:

> "Mr. President, right now, the Obama Administration is in the process of negotiating what might prove to be the most far-reaching economic agreement since the World Trade Organization was established nearly twenty years ago. The goal of this agreement – known as the Trans Pacific Partnership, TPP – is to economically bind together the economies of the Asia Pacific. It involves countries ranging from Australia, Singapore, Vietnam, Peru, Chile and the United States and holds the potential to include many more countries, like Japan, Korea, Canada, and Mexico.
>
> If successful, the agreement will set norms for the trade of goods and services and includes disciplines related to intellectual property, access to medicines, Internet governance, investment, government procurement, worker rights and environmental standards. If agreed to, TPP will set the tone for our nation's economic future for years to come, impacting the way Congress intervenes and acts on behalf of the American people it represents.
>
> It may be the U.S. Trade Representative's, USTR, current job to negotiate trade agreements on behalf of the United States, but Article I Section 8 of the U.S. Constitution gives Congress – not the USTR or any other member of the Executive Branch – the responsibility of regulating foreign commerce. It was our Founding Fathers' intention to ensure that the laws and policies that govern the American people take into account the interests of all the American people, not just a privileged few.
>
> Yet, the majority of Congress is being kept in the dark as to the substance of the TPP negotiations, while representatives of U.S. corporations – like Halliburton, Chevron, PHRMA, Comcast, and the Motion Picture Association of America – are being consulted and made privy to details of the agreement. As the Office of the USTR will tell you, the President gives it broad

power to keep information about the trade policies it advances and negotiates, secret. Let me tell you, the USTR is making full use of this authority.

As the Chairman of the Senate Finance Committee's Subcommittee on International Trade, Customs, and Global Competitiveness, my office is responsible for conducting oversight over the USTR and trade negotiations. To do that, I asked that my staff obtain the proper security credentials to view the information that USTR keeps confidential and secret. This is material that fully describes what the USTR is seeking in the TPP talks on behalf of the American people and on behalf of Congress. More than two months after receiving the proper security credentials, my staff is still barred from viewing the details of the proposals that USTR is advancing.

We hear that the process by which TPP is being negotiated has been a model of transparency. I disagree with that statement. And not just because the Staff Director of the Senate subcommittee responsible for oversight of international trade continues to be denied access to substantive and detailed information that pertains to the TPP talks. Congress passed legislation in 2002 to form the Congressional Oversight Group, or COG, to foster more USTR consultation with Congress. I was a senator in 2002. I voted for that law and I can tell you the intention of that law was to ensure that USTR consulted with more Members of Congress not less.

In trying to get to the bottom of why my staff is being denied information, it seems that some in the Executive Branch may be interpreting the law that established the COG to mean that only the few Members of Congress who belong to the COG can be given access to trade negotiation information, while every other Member of Congress, and their staff, must be denied such access.

So, this is not just a question of whether or not cleared staff should have access to information about the TPP talks, this is a question of whether or not the administration believes that most Members of Congress can or should have a say in trade negotiations.

Again, having voted for that law, I strongly disagree with such an interpretation and find it offensive that some would suggest that a law meant to foster more consultation with Congress is intended to limit it.

But given that the TPP negotiations are currently underway and I – and the vast majority of my colleagues and their staff – continue to be denied a full understanding of what the USTR is seeking in the agreement, we do not have time to waste on a protracted legal battle over this issue. Therefore, I am introducing legislation to clarify the intent of the COG statute. The legislation, I propose, is straightforward. It gives all Members of Congress and staff with appropriate clearance access to the substance of trade negotiations. Finally, Members of Congress who are responsible for conducting oversight over the enforcement of trade agreements will be provided information by the Executive Branch indicating whether our trading partners are living up to their trade obligations. Put simply, this legislation would ensure that the representatives elected by the American people are afforded the same level of influence over our nation's policies as the paid representatives of PHRMA, Halliburton and the Motion Picture Association."

While the Constitution designates Congress as the body with authority over the substance of U.S. international commercial policy, the steady erosion of Congress' authority after 40 years of Fast Track has culminated in negotiations on the largest, most impactful agreement in decades hurtling towards conclusion with Congress altogether sidelined. The executive branch's disregard for the constitutional role of Congress in the process has reached such extremes that executive branch negotiators have systematically disregarded the views of bipartisan blocs of House and Senate members. The members have launched flotillas of letters to the president and USTR on issues ranging from the failure of USTR to include disciplines against currency manipulation despite years of congressional demands[285] to the TPP's inclusion of a chapter on immigration visas[286] to threats to end-run Congress' 2012 rejection of the Stop Online Piracy Act (SOPA) – legislation that many deemed a threat to Internet freedom and innovation – by inclusion of core aspects of the failed legislation in the TPP's copyright chapter.[287]

Also ignored have been congressional interventions aimed at getting executive branch negotiators to alter U.S. proposals that threaten imported food safety (and could undermine the 2011-enacted Food Safety Modernization Act),[288] proposals that would ban Buy American procurement preferences supported by overwhelming majorities of Americans,[289] and proposals that would roll back medicine patent reforms made by the Bush II administration.[290] The bipartisan National Conference of State Legislatures, which represents the 50 U.S. state legislatures, has joined the fray – passing a formal resolution announcing it would oppose any agreement that includes the NAFTA-style investor-state regime that submits the United States to the jurisdiction of foreign tribunals, which the Obama administration insists be included in the TPP.[291]

The Obama administration's imperial approach to TPP, the largest and most impactful trade agreement in decades, is the dangerous but not unforeseeable result of the legacy of Fast Track. But, the administration's conduct, premised on the assumption that Congress has ceded its constitutional trade policy role, in fact relies on Congress' continued willingness to do so.

---

285. See, for example, Franken, et al., 2012.
286. See, for example, Conyers and Smith, 2012.
287. See, for example, Lofgren, 2012.
288. See, for example, DeLauro, 2011.
289. See, for example, Edwards, et al., 2012.
290. See, for example, Waxman, 2012.
291. NCSL, 2012. "NCSL will not support Bilateral Investment Treaties (BITs) or Free Trade Agreements (FTAs) with investment chapters that provide greater substantive or procedural rights to foreign companies than U.S. companies enjoy under the U.S. Constitution. Specifically, NCSL will not support any BIT or FTA that provides for investor/state dispute resolution."

Unless Congress gives it authority to do so, the Obama administration cannot sign a TPP that submits the United States to the jurisdiction of foreign tribunals, bans Buy American procurement preferences, includes an entire chapter on immigration policy, and fails to discipline currency manipulation despite key TPP countries' established track record of using this tactic. And only with an explicit delegation by Congress of its constitutional authority can the executive branch once again use Fast Track to sign the TPP without congressional approval, thereby circumventing congressional opposition to elements of SOPA and other TPP-enshrined policies Congress has previously rejected.

The administration is operating with disdain for Congress' role – as if a Fast Track-style broad delegation of congressional trade authority is permanently in effect – because it assumes that Congress will eventually take action to make this a legal reality. After four decades of Fast Track, Democratic and Republican administrations alike have become addicted to this extraordinary power, and predictably so. Given the expansive scope of the policies now set in "trade" agreements and the permanence of such terms, the executive branch's ability to control unilaterally the agreements' contents provides it with a powerful means to determine wide swaths of American policy without the difficult compromises and consensus-building that are fundamental to democratic governance. While this reality may now be most troubling to conservative members of Congress concerned with what a Democratic president may use this power to achieve over their opposition, the problem is a structural one, with deep institutional implications for American governance in this era of globalization.

Yet, this is a problem that is entirely within Congress' ability to remedy. Congress is in no way bound to accept the Constitution-defying legacy of Fast Track in general, nor as it is playing out in the context of TPP negotiations. With respect to the TPP, Congress could simply notify the executive branch that it will cut off funding for TPP negotiations unless and until the executive branch shares draft TPP negotiating texts with all of the congressional committees whose jurisdiction is implicated (which is most committees). Each committee could call oversight hearings on the chapters of the agreement that would set policy under each committee's jurisdiction, and demand a full accounting by the administration.

But, while reasserting this level of congressional involvement is critical, it is not sufficient.

A structural fix is needed to remedy a structural problem: the absence of a 21st century process for congressional-executive coordination on trade agreement negotiations. Congress requires a new mechanism to manage executive branch trade negotiators. This new mechanism must provide a level of accountability appropriate to the enormous impact that today's "trade" agreements can have on sweeping expanses of critical, domestic non-trade federal and state policy. Congress must design a new mechanism to replace Fast Track – one that carefully delineates the role of the executive branch in trade negotiations, takes into account the scope of today's "trade" agreements and restores Congress' ability to fulfill its constitutional authority with respect to controlling the content of American trade policy.

As we turn to the conclusion of this book, which explores alternatives to Fast Track that could achieve trade expansion without undermining the key tenets of American constitutional governance, the fundamental question, which has enormous political and policy implications, is: *will* Congress act to reassert its constitutional rights over trade policy?

Conclusion: Toward A New Consensus

This book details how the U.S. trade-agreement negotiation and approval process has developed over time and has been altered by Congress to accommodate changing circumstances. Such changes are both natural and inevitable.

Because the Constitution gives Congress exclusive authority to set tariff rates and to decide the terms of commerce with foreign nations, while granting authority to the executive branch to conduct international negotiations, some form of coordination is required. Over the course of the United States' existence, this constitutional separation of powers has resulted in the legislative and executive branch playing widely varying roles in the formation of both trade agreements and trade policy more generally. One constant has been the executive branch's attempts to acquire increased control over these matters.

In the Republic's first 100 years, trade agreements were generally adopted by the Senate as treaties, with bicameral legislation used to implement the changes to U.S. tariff rates. From 1890 to 1934, Congress experimented with delegating defined authority to negotiate tariff terms to the executive branch. The first several delegations allowed the executive to negotiate tariff agreements without subsequent congressional approval, but these were limited to specific countries and goods. The 1922 act introduced the notion of allowing the executive to proclaim tariff adjustments to equalize the costs of production across countries. Several acts during the period authorized the president to negotiate trade agreements, while requiring that these agreements be brought back to Congress for approval.

With the 1934 Reciprocal Trade Agreements Act (RTAA), Congress permitted the executive to negotiate trade agreements (which modified tariffs within certain bands) without a congressional implementing vote. The act was controversial in Congress, and was initially established only as an emergency measure for three years, with any agreements negotiated without Congress' approval terminating with the authority itself.

However, once established, the RTAA's tariff proclamation authority was repeatedly extended by Congress for one- to three-year periods. Scores of trade agreements were completed under this form of tariff-proclamation authority, including the original 1947 GATT and four rounds of further GATT negotiations. The GATT set certain principles regarding trade in goods and established tariff rates. Congress did not vote on the GATT rounds, and a proposal to establish an International Trade Organization (which would house the GATT) failed to obtain Senate treaty approval. By 1958, as the importance of trade to the U.S. economy increased, Congress reasserted its role by establishing a form of legislative veto.

When the Johnson administration overstepped its congressionally-delegated tariff authority in the 1967 GATT Kennedy Round, Congress ended its willingness to allow adoption of trade agreements without an *affirmative* congressional vote. That GATT pact included non-tariff measures related to anti-dumping policy. Congress had warned that such matters related to domestic law, not tariffs, and were outside of the executive's trade authority. Johnson signed the agreement anyway. Congress demonstrated its constitutional prerogatives by refusing to implement that aspect of the GATT deal, while Johnson used existing tariff-proclamation authority to implement the Kennedy Round tariff cuts. Congress did not provide any new delegation of presidential trade authority from 1967 to 1975.

Fast Track was the next mechanism for U.S. trade-agreement negotiation and approval. During President Nixon's narrowly-won first term, he worked to consolidate his political base by courting various constituencies with import-restraining measures. After winning his second term, Nixon changed his economic team, but continued prioritizing political power over policy substance. His initial proposal for new presidential trade authority would have allowed him to negotiate trade agreements on tariff and certain non-tariff issues such as procurement and dumping; he would also be able to *proclaim* not only the new tariff rates, *but the changes to federal law needed to implement the pacts.*

The Nixon administration initially argued that this was necessary to bring other countries to the negotiating table after the Kennedy Round meltdown. However, when countries agreed to launch the next GATT Tokyo Round prior to any delegation of congressional trade authority, the administration conceded that the real issue was ensuring a final vote on trade agreements. The Senate put a stop to Nixon's outlandish (and almost certainly unconstitutional) proposal that would have taken over Congress' basic legislative authority. However, the Senate did agree to a Fast Track system that would allow the president to negotiate on tariff and certain non-tariff issues and sign and enter into agreements *before* a congressional vote, with a later vote guaranteed on the already signed pacts within a set amount of time under controlled floor-voting rules. The Nixon administration pledged that the non-tariff authority would be used only on matters closely related to trade, such as anti-dumping provisions.

The GATT Tokyo Round was completed under this form of Fast Track. For the first time, it included "codes" on issues traditionally under sole congressional purview, such as procurement, non-tariff barriers (i.e. domestic regulatory standards) and dumping. The Fast Track authority was extended for an additional eight years in 1979.

The Reagan administration transformed Nixon's consolidation of presidential *trade-* agreement power into a new instrument expanding presidential power over an array of new *non-trade* policy matters, using trade agreements to facilitate backdoor domestic implementation of proposals that were controversial at home. This form of diplomatic legislating was then used by later Democratic and Republican presidents to lock in U.S. immigration policies at the WTO, among other uses of trade negotiations by presidents to evade congressional authority over non-trade matters. The 1984 and 1988 Fast Tracks first authorized a U.S. president to negotiate and enter into agreements that set international rules for service-sector, intellectual property, financial and investment policy, constraining the domestic policy space of Congress and preempting state policies. This extraordinary, new expansion of presidential authority – which allowed the branch to diplomatically legislate on a broad array of domestic non-trade issues – was used to launch the Uruguay Round GATT talks in 1986.

The first President Bush's notice to Congress of his intent to use

Fast Track to launch NAFTA negotiations with Mexico triggered a congressional backlash against Fast Track. In 1991, fair traders and constitutionalists invoked a midterm Fast Track extension disapproval procedure that provided for a congressional a vote to terminate Fast Track authority. Unlike the near-unanimous bipartisan passage of the 1979, 1984 and 1988 Fast Tracks, 192 House members voted against Fast Track under the disapproval resolution. But without a majority to stop its extension, the procedure remained in effect for use to finalize NAFTA. In 1993, a WTO-specific Fast Track extension was obtained by the Clinton administration.

NAFTA and the WTO exploded the boundaries of "trade" agreements. These pacts established numerous constraints and obligations on a wide range of policies unrelated to trade – from immigration and food safety, to drug patents and truck safety. Unlike the widely supported GATT Tokyo Round, the WTO and NAFTA engendered fierce bipartisan congressional opposition. Their approval required a great deal of the Clinton administration's political capital. Yet even the critics of NAFTA and the WTO did not understand the full impacts of the agreements' expansive non-tariff terms until the pacts began to undermine an array of domestic non-trade laws. And despite promises by the pacts' supporters that the deals would reverse the growing U.S. trade deficit, U.S. trade with Mexico shifted from balance to a growing deficit, as the U.S. global trade deficit continued to grow. Congress' support for Fast Track – and the expansive international commercial agreements it had wrought – steadily diminished. Meanwhile, U.S. public opinion about NAFTA-style agreements grew increasingly negative on a transpartisan basis.

A key feature of Fast Track was that Congress' stated negotiating objectives were not binding on executive branch negotiators. Because the president could sign and enter into an agreement before Congress voted, Congress retained no leverage to ensure that its objectives were met. Thus, for instance, the Omnibus Trade and Competitiveness Act of 1988 – which included the Fast Track delegation used for NAFTA and the WTO – included negotiating objectives that labor standards be included in trade agreements. However, labor provisions were not included in either NAFTA or the WTO. Then in later years, the most robust labor standards ever included in a U.S. trade agreement were added to four George W. Bush-negotiated trade agreements with Colombia, Korea, Panama and Peru. This addition occurred despite the fact that these pacts had been negotiated under a Fast Track that explicitly limited inclusion of such terms.

The Clinton administration, known for its successful trade-expansion agenda, did not have Fast Track authority for six of its eight years. It implemented numerous trade agreements without the extraordinary delegation of Congress' authority. Indeed, a Fast Track bill for the Clinton administration was voted down on the House floor in 1998 – a historic first. From 1995 through 2002, there was no congressional delegation of trade authority, even as U.S. trade expanded significantly.

President George W. Bush came to office with top priorities that included the establishment of Fast Track and the expansion of NAFTA. After a lengthy battle, he obtained a Fast Track delegation in 2002. Many Democrats who had ardently supported past Fast Tracks led the fight against this one, citing the implications of providing the executive branch with enormous authority to implement non-trade policies that would normally be considered the jurisdiction of the legislative branch and state legislatures. Sizeable blocs of House GOP voted against this delegation of Fast Track, which passed by one vote. Bush used Fast Track to extend the NAFTA model through eight pacts, including CAFTA, which passed by a two-vote margin in 2005.

Ironically, it was Bush's use of Fast Track's full powers that destroyed what was left of congressional support for the extraordinary procedure. The Bush administration dispensed with many of the traditional, albeit not required, executive-legislative coordination practices. Instead of negotiating with the trade gatekeeper committees on a bipartisan basis, the Bush administration even ignored a unanimously supported Finance Committee amendment passed in the Oman FTA's mock mark up in 2006. On the Peru FTA, the executive stretched even further, first cutting a deal with Democratic congressional trade leaders to add improved labor and other provisions to the already signed agreement, and then renegotiating these terms of the signed agreements with Peru, Panama, and Colombia without providing Congress with the required notice of intent to enter into an agreement. This left some Republicans fuming and voting no on the deal's mock mark up. (In the last days of his term, Bush then angered Rangel and Levin by implementing the deal before Peru had made the changes to its domestic laws required to meet the labor and environmental improvements the Democrats had obtained in the FTA's text.)

The final straw came when Bush used the Fast Track process to try to force a vote on the Colombia FTA in April 2008, after congressional leaders had explicitly asked for further discussion of the proposal. Congress reasserted its constitutional prerogatives and passed a new rule that removed the pact from the 60-day House vote timetable. For Fast Track's critics, this string of executive abuses only confirmed their long-time warnings.

Candidate Barack Obama had criticized Fast Track in the presidential primaries, describing reforms he would implement to create a new way for Congress and the executive branch to coordinate on trade agreement negotiations and approvals. While strong opposition to three Bush-signed FTAs led to the deals being pushed to the back burner for Obama's first term, in 2011 he nonetheless used (and some would say abused, given changes made to the Korea FTA after Fast Track had expired) Fast Track procedures to ram through three trade deals to which enhanced labor standards had been added *post facto*.

The Obama administration has made negotiation of the Trans-Pacific Partnership pact its top trade priority and has conducted 16 rounds of negotiations over the past three years. However, the Obama administration has not requested a new delegation of trade authority, even though its USTR regularly mentioned the eventual plan to so do. Notably, the administration's lack of Fast Track has not hindered it from vigorously negotiating the deal.

However, years of Congress abandoning its constitutional prerogatives on trade has led the Obama administration to conduct TPP negotiations as if Article I-Section 8 of the U.S. Constitution, which provides Congress with exclusive authority over the content of American trade policy, did not exist. While administration officials have conducted briefings for congressional staff and responded to requests to meet with members of Congress about the TPP, the administration has not provided Congress with access to what is now a draft composite bracketed text of the massive agreement. Indeed, the administration has announced its plans to complete the agreement in the fall of 2013. Some Members of Congress and congressional staff have even been denied access to the U.S. proposals submitted for the negotiations. Even the chairman of the Senate Finance Trade Subcommittee, which has formal jurisdiction over the pact, has been denied access to draft TPP texts, which led him to submit legislation requiring the administration to provide such access. The Obama administration also has terminated the past practice of allowing congressional observers to attend the trade negotiating rounds. This conduct, coming on the heels of President Bush's revealing "full use" of Fast Track's powers with respect to the Colombia FTA, does not create a hospitable environment for an eventual administration request for Congress to delegate legally its constitutional trade authority through a broad mechanism similar to past Fast Track delegations.

Yet, the Obama administration might find more congressional support for a new trade authority mechanism that incorporates Obama's 2008 Fast Track reform proposals and builds on past congressional reform proposals. As noted above, President Barack Obama promised to "replace Fast Track with a process that includes criteria determining appropriate negotiating partners ... I will ensure that Congress plays a strong and informed role in our international economic policy and in any future agreements we pursue and in our efforts to amend existing agreements."[292]

Indeed, as this book's review of the five past systems of trade authority delegation shows, each prior mechanism was eventually overtaken by changes in external realities – the changing scope of the subject matter being negotiated in "trade" deals – and changes in Congress' political tolerance for the institutional problems caused by each regime.

---

292. Obama, 2007.

The Fast Track mechanism was but one of various procedures employed by Congress to coordinate trade-agreement negotiations and approval. As President Kennedy noted in 1961, an old delegation method that does not meet the needs of its era "must not simply be renewed, it must be replaced."

This review has also shown that the Fast Track mechanism was not necessary to ensure U.S. trade agreements or trade expansion. Under other delegations – or in the absence of delegations – trade has expanded and agreements have been signed, negotiated and put into effect. For instance, while the Clinton administration was without Fast Track, trade expanded over 30 percent from 1995 to 2000. And by its own reckoning, the Clinton administration negotiated and passed 130 trade and investment agreements without Fast Track, including the Jordan FTA, which passed under normal congressional floor procedures. Additionally, the China WTO accession agreement (which was the basis for Congress' approval of permanent most favored nation treatment for China) passed under regular congressional procedures. As Rep. Becerra pointed out in the 2001 floor debate on Fast Track "Over the past 250 years of our Nation's existence, for only 20 of those years, from 1974 to 1994, has this body granted the President authority for fast tracking any trade agreement. In those 20 years, five agreements were signed. In contrast, during the 8 years of the Clinton administration, 300 agreements were signed with countries from Belarus to Japan to Uzbekistan. We can do this without Fast Track."

We have also described the mismatch between the Fast Track mechanism and the challenges of today's complex international commercial agreements. Fast Track was premised on 1970s realities, when trade agreements were still largely about traditional trade matters such as tariffs, quotas and anti-dumping policy. Unless Congress forbids the inclusion of binding rules on non-trade policy issues such as patents, immigration, service-sector and procurement policy, in trade-agreement negotiations altogether, it will need a greatly enhanced role in formulating and reviewing trade-pact terms.

Specifically, this means the legislative branch must determine what non-trade matters can and cannot be included in international commercial pacts. In addition to considerations of policy space – for instance excluding certain matters to preserve flexibility to modify non-trade policies as circumstances require without having to obtain agreement by all trade partner countries to amend trade pacts – Congress must also have the capacity to ensure that non-trade regulatory provisions are consistent with domestic policy goals. Ensuring Congress can hold executive-branch negotiators accountable to legislative directives will require changes to the delegation mechanism at the core of Fast Track, not just the addition of new negotiating objectives that have been systematically ignored under past delegations.

Even defenders of current trade policies agree that Fast Track's time has passed, and a new delegation mechanism is needed. Hal Shapiro, the author of a recent book on the topic, wrote that Fast Track "is surely not what the drafters of the Constitution intended. Indeed, in key respects, Fast Track appears to contravene what they intended. Moreover, it is not necessary, and it does not promote the right debate… Fast Track has become a distraction for fashioning policy to a national globalization strategy."[293] And arch-free market advocate and former Sen. Phil Gramm (R-Texas) has said that he opposes any delegation of Fast Track that includes labor and environmental standards, precisely because he views these as domestic in nature. "If we had a President who wanted to change environmental or labor law, and do it in a way to limit congressional power and authority, he could do it unilaterally through Fast Track." (Interestingly, he views the inclusion of non-trade patent terms in Fast Tracked trade deals as acceptable, because "America is in the patent and copyright business… I would argue that element in free trade agreements was pretty much like Britain being for freedom of the seas when they controlled the seas because they had the world's greatest navy.") Even if one doesn't agree with his conclusions on substance with respect to what is and is not related to trade, Gramm's notion of how Fast Track facilitates unilateral executive branch policymaking is sound.

293. Shapiro, 2006, at 161-162.

Some observers will always think that *any* congressional or public input on trade is too much. For instance, one Clinton (and then Obama) administration official, Harold Koh, called Fast Track "the most congressionally influenced trade regime since Smoot-Hawley." Indeed, he wrote that even the 1962 act offered Congress "too much input."[294] Invariably, when any new congressional trade delegation mechanism is brought up, those who benefited from Fast Track's allocation of decision-making power will attack the new proposal – probably as "protectionist." However, history has shown trade expansion to flourish under a variety of institutional arrangements. This is not a battle between protectionism and free trade. Rather, at issue is Congress' appropriate role in devising international commercial agreements that deeply affect and sometimes directly conflict with a wide range of non-trade domestic policy. This is a fundamental question of the practice of democratic governance in our era of globalization.

The quest for the next trade-authority system has already begun. Starting in 2007 when the last grant of Fast Track terminated, prominent private sector groups representing diverse interests passed formal policy resolutions and issued papers laying out their views of the core requirements for any new trade authority. Many of these proposals built off of those offered in the past by members of Congress, such as the 1995 Fast Track replacement proposal promoted by Rep. Bill Richardson and Minority Leader Richard Gephardt,[295] and the 2001-02 Rangel-Levin-Matsui Fast Track reform proposal.

In 2007 and 2008 the AFL-CIO and Change to Win labor federations and the National Farmers Union passed formal policy resolutions calling on Congress to replace Fast Track with a mechanism that enhances Congress' role. These resolutions contemplate the inclusion of readiness criteria, binding negotiating objectives, and pre-signing votes on trade-agreement contents – areas described in more detail below. Public Citizen and other organizations have called for a new trade negotiation system based on similar elements.[296]

---

294. Koh, 1986, at 1202, 1208 and 1211.
295. IUT, 1995b.
296. Copies of these resolutions are available at: http://www.citizen.org/trade/fasttrack/.

Perhaps the clearest evidence that the Fast Track delegation system has altogether lost its legitimacy has been the reform proposals of business interests who have long defended the status quo. The National Foreign Trade Council (NFTC), which represents the interests of large corporations who had a privileged role in shaping U.S. trade agreements under previous delegations, released a model "Trade Negotiation Authority Act of 2009" in late 2008. It maintains the old Fast Track structure, but even so includes certain enhancements in Congress' role, such as establishment of a congressional super-committee that would be required to approve executive-branch proposals to launch FTA talks with specific countries. This Joint Committee on Trade would be comprised of chairs and ranking members of an array of committees whose jurisdiction is affected by today's wide-ranging "trade" agreements, included the chairman and ranking members of the Ways and Means and Finance Committees plus three additional members from each, and the chairman and ranking members of the Agriculture, Energy and Commerce, Financial Services, Foreign Affairs, Judiciary, Small Business, Banking, Commerce, and Foreign Relations committees, plus three additional members designated by each body's leadership, two from the majority and one from the minority.[297]

Interestingly, establishment of such a trade super-committee is one element of a comprehensive U.S. trade reform proposal that was introduced into Congress in 2009. The Trade Reform, Accountability, Development and Employment (TRADE) Act (S. 2821/ H.R. 3012) introduced by Sen. Sherrod Brown (D-Ohio) and Rep. Mike Michaud (D-Maine) set forth the principles for a Fast Track replacement and also detailed mandatory objectives with which new and existing U.S. trade deals must comply. At the end of the 111th Congress, the House bill had 146 bipartisan cosponsors, including 13 Committee chairs and 57 Subcommittee chairs of diverse geographic and political provenance.[298] The Fast Track replacement proposal in these bills built on past congressional reform efforts and the proposals of various academics and civil society groups. It included:

---

297. NFTC, 2008.
298. Information about the TRADE Act (H.R. 6180) is available at http://thomas.loc.gov/.

- Specific "readiness criteria" set by Congress for selecting future U.S. trade negotiating partners. In order for the president to initiate negotiations, the Ways & Means and Finance committees must confirm that countries with whom the executive proposes to negotiate meet Congress' statutory readiness criteria;

- Mandatory congressional negotiating objectives that list what must be and must not be included in future trade agreements;

- Enhanced consultations with (and briefings of) Congress by executive branch trade officials throughout the negotiating process;

- Creation of a Congressional Trade Agreement Review Committee that includes the chair and ranking member of House and Senate committee whose jurisdiction is directly covered by today's international commercial agreements. This committee is designed to supplement the role of the gatekeeper committees, by providing a mechanism for legislators with expertise in the non-trade issues covered by the pacts to access trade briefings and provide input to executive-branch officials;

- Certification by the Congressional Trade Agreement Review Committee that mandatory negotiating objectives have been met *before* a trade agreement can be brought to a vote. This would ensure that executive-branch negotiators – and their counterparts from other countries – have an incentive to meet Congress' negotiating objectives;

- A congressional *pre-signing* vote to approve an agreement's text and explicitly authorize the president to sign and enter into it. This critical measure would ensure that Congress can review and decide on the merits of an agreement before it is signed. This would also create a strong disincentive for executive-branch negotiators to try to use trade pacts to push non-trade measures otherwise opposed by Congress. It would also allow Congress a real say in the contents of agreements when changes can still be made, if necessary. Because Congress would have the opportunity up front to ensure that pacts and negotiating partners meet their criteria, voting on final implementing legislation would no longer become a high-stakes proxy for non-implementation-related disagreements;

- A process to provide subfederal officials a role in deciding whether their states will agree to be bound to trade pacts' non-trade policy obligations and constraints regarding land-use, service-sector, procurement, and investment policies. However, unlike the Bricker Amendment in the 1950s (or the Articles of Confederation in the 1780s), this mechanism would not block the federal government from adopting international agreements or trade policies within its jurisdiction.

In the 112th Congress, Senator Brown introduced the 21st Century Trade Agreement and Market Access Act (S. 3347), which included a similar Fast Track replacement proposal.

Arguments for restoring Congress' authority and increasing democratic participation in the trade policymaking process are compelling. While perfect democratic debate about globalization policy is impossible, a bias toward the inclusion of more voices is likely to result in a better representation of the national interest.[299] Further, the expansive non-trade scope of today's international commercial agreements argues for Congress to have a more prominent role in their negotiation and approval than ever before in the nation's history.

One Fast Track advocate hit the nail on the head when he wrote,

> "the president is well-situated to accumulate foreign affairs power [while Congress is not]. Congress thus could benefit by utilizing tools that would redress the balance-of-powers weakness vis-à-vis the executive."[300]

Elements of such redress would include a trade-authority mechanism broken up into stages of executive-legislative cooperation, over which the Congress retains leverage – and indeed control – regarding whether the next stage of delegation is provided. In addition, a process

299. Goodin, 2007.
300. Carrier, 1996, at 694-695.

that recognizes the broad scope of today's international commercial negotiations through greater and more diverse congressional involvement could redress the current power imbalance.

As this review has shown, delegation of Congress' trade authority has taken different forms over the course of the nation's history, with a new system of delegation being established every few decades since 1890 in response to changing circumstances. The next few years will show whether the U.S. political system is sufficiently dynamic to embrace a change towards a new delegation mechanism, one that reduces political tension about trade policy and secures prosperity for the greatest number of Americans, while preserving the vital tenets of American democracy in the era of globalization.

References

Abrams, Jim. "Democrats, Bush Reach Trade Framework," *Associated Press*, May 10, 2007.

Ackerman, Bruce, and David Golove, "Is NAFTA Constitutional?" *Harvard Law Review*, 108:4, February 1995.

AP. "U.S. officials reach agreement on trade deals," *Associated Press*, May 10, 2007.

Baker, Dean. *The United States Since 1980*, (Cambridge: Cambridge University Press, 2007).

Bardwell, Kedron. "The Puzzling Decline in House Support for Free Trade: Was Fast Track a Referendum on NAFTA," *Legislative Studies Quarterly*, 25:4, November 2000.

Barlow, Maude. *The Fight of My Life*, (Toronto: Harper Collins, 1998.)

BDG. "Trade a Chaos," *Boston Daily Globe*, Sept. 28, 1890.

Beckman, Aldo. "Nixon Turning to Trade as World Power Force," *Chicago Tribune*, Dec. 3, 1972.

Berger, Marilyn. "Hill Panel Agrees on Trade Powers," *Washington Post*, Sept. 15, 1973.

Bergsten, C. Fred. "The new economics and U.S. foreign policy," *Foreign Affairs*, January 1972.

Bergsten, C. Fred. "The Democrats' Dangerous Trade Games," *Wall Street Journal*, May 20, 2008.

Biglaiser, Glen, and David J. Jackson and Jeffrey S. Peake, "Back on Track: Support for Presidential Trade Authority in the House of Representatives," *American Politics Research*, 32, 2004.

Biven, W. Carl. *Jimmy Carter's Economy*, (Chapel Hill: University of North Carolina Press, 2002).

Bivens, Josh. "Trade, jobs and wages," Economic Policy Institute Issue Brief, May 6, 2008. Available at: http://www.epi.org/content.cfm/ib244. Accessed July 25, 2008.

Blinkhorn, Laura. "Lack of Quorum Delays Action on Trade Bills," *Congressional Quarterly Committee Coverage*, July 27, 2006.

Blustein, Paul. "Zoellick's Aggressive Push for Trade Bill Draws Fire," *Washington Post*, Oct. 23, 2001.

Bolle, Mary Jane. "Jordan-U.S. Free Trade Agreement: Labor Issues," Congressional Research Service Report RS20968, July 15, 2003. Available at: http://assets.opencrs.com/rpts/RS20968_20030715.pdf. Accessed July 22, 2008.

Bottari, Mary, and Lori Wallach. "NAFTA's Threat to Sovereignty and Democracy: The Record of NAFTA Chapter 11 Investor-State Cases 1994-2005," Public Citizen Report, February 2005. Available at: http://www.citizen.org/documents/Chapter%2011%20Report%20 Final.pdf. Accessed July 21, 2008.

Bottari, Mary, and Lori Wallach. "States' Rights and International Trade: A Legislator's Guide to Reinvigorating Federalism in the Era of Globalization," Public Citizen Report, February 2007. Available at: http://www.citizen.org/documents/Guide_2.9_Final.pdf. Accessed July 21, 2008.

Bottari, Mary. "Trade Deficit in Food Safety," Public Citizen Report, July 2007. Available at: http://www.citizen.org/publications/release.cfm?ID=7535&secID=2354&cat ID=126. Accessed July 22, 2008.

Bottari, Mary, and Lori Wallach. "Federalism and Global Governance: Comparative Analysis of Trade Agreement Negotiation and Approval Mechanisms Used in U.S. and Other Federalist Governance Systems," Public Citizen, July 2008. "Prosperity Undermined During Era of Fast Tracked NAFTA and WTO Model Trade Agreements," Public Citizen, 2013. Available at http://www.citizen.org/documents/federalism.pdf.

Bradsher, Keith. "Whoops! It's 1985 all over again," *New York Times*, Dec. 19, 2004.

Caro, Robert A. *Master of the Senate*, (New York: Vintage, 2002).

Carrier, Michael A. "All aboard the presidential fast track: from trade to beyond," *George Washington Journal of International Law & Economy*, 29, 1996.

Carter, Dan. *The Politics of Rage*, (Baton Rouge: Louisiana State University Press, 1995).

CDT. "Reciprocity with Hawaii," *Chicago Daily Tribune*, Feb. 5, 1875.

Chang, Ha-Joon. *Bad Samaritans*, (New York: Bloomsbury Press, 2008).

Charnovitz, Steve. "Book Review of Shapiro," *Journal of International Economic Law*, 1-9, 2007.

Chorev, Nitsan. *Remaking U.S. Trade Policy: From Protectionism to Globalization*, (Ithaca Cornell University Press, 2007).

Claybrook, Joan. Statement to House Committee on Appropriations, Public Citizen, March 8, 2007. Available at: http://www.citizen.org/documents/2007-03-claybrook-testimony-nafta-trucks.pdf. Accessed July 29, 2008.

Cloud, David S. "Democrats Weigh the Politics of Battling Bush and Mexico," *Congressional Quarterly*, 49:660, 1991.

Conconi, Paola, and Giovanni Facchini and Maurizio Zanardi, "Fast Track Authority and International Trade Negotiations," Centre for Economic Policy Research Discussion Paper 6790, April 2008.

Conley, Richard S. "Derailing presidential fast-track authority," *Political Research Quarterly*, 52:4, December 1999.

Conyers, John and Lamar Smith. Letter from Reps. John Conyers and Lamar Smith to U.S. Trade Representative Ron Kirk, March 5, 2012.

CT. "Clinton Pardons 59 including Chicago's Dan Rostenkowski," *Chicago Tribune*, Dec. 22, 2000.

Dale, Jr., Edwin L. "Severs link between dollar and gold," *New York Times*, Aug. 16, 1971.

Dale, Jr., Edwin L. "Urgency Stressed," *New York Times*, April 11, 1973.

DeLauro, Rosa. Letter from Rep. Rosa DeLauro to U.S. Trade Representative Ron Kirk, Sep. 7, 2011. Available at: http://delauro.house.gov/index.php?option=com_content&view=article&id=406:-delauro-food-safety-critical-issue-in-upcoming-trade-talks&catid=7:2011-press-releases&Itemid=23. Accessed Feb. 26, 2013.

Destler, I.M. *American Trade Politics* (Washington, D.C.: Institute for International Economics, 2005).

Drajem, Mark. "Democrats, Unions Push Plan to Review, Overhaul Trade Accords," Bloomberg, June 4, 2008.

Drake, William J., and Kalypso Nicolaidis. "Ideas, Interests, and Institutionalization: 'Trade in Services' and the Uruguay Round," *International Organization*, Vol. 46, No. 1, Knowledge, Power, and International Policy Coordination, Winter 1992.

Dunne, Nancy. "Fears Over "GATTzilla, the Trade Monster," *Financial Times*, Jan. 30, 1992.

Ehrlich, Sean D. "The Fair Trade Challenge to Embedded Liberalism," Florida State University Paper, September 2008.

Eichengreen, Barry, and Douglas A. Irwin. "International Economic Policy: Was There a Bush Doctrine?" NBER Working Paper 13831, March 2008.

Engel, Steven T. and David J. Jackson. "Wielding the Stick Instead of the Carrot: Labor PAC Punishment of Pro-NAFTA Democrats," *Political Research Quarterly* 51:3, September 1998.

Engler, Mark. *How to Rule the World,* (New York: Nation Books, 2008).

Eckes, Jr., Alfred E. *Opening America's Market: U.S. Foreign Trade Policy Since 1776,* (Chapel Hill: University of North Carolina Press, 1995).

Edwards, Donna, et al. Letter from 69 members of Congress to President Barack Obama, May 3, 2012. Available at: http://donnaedwards.house.gov/uploads/Buy%20American%20TPP%20 Ltr%20to%20Admin.pdf.

Farnsworth, Clyde H. "Battles loom over imports," *New York Times,* April 8, 1985a.

Farnsworth, Clyde H. "Anti-import bills regain momentum," *New York Times,* Sept. 13, 1985b.

Faux, Jeff. *The Global Class War,* (New York: Wiley, 2006).

Forbes, Lauren. Memo on Disapproval Resolutions, Public Citizen, July 2008. Available at: www.citizen.org/documents/forbes.pdf.

Franken, Al, et al. Letter from 24 Senators to President Barack Obama, Dec. 3, 2012. Available at: http://www.franken.senate.gov/?p=hot_topic&id=2241. Accessed Feb. 26, 2013.

Gannon, James. "Nixon Asks Broad Authority to Reduce Barriers," *Wall Street Journal,* April 11, 1973.

GAO. "An Analysis of Free Trade Agreements and Congressional and Private Sector Consultations Under Trade Promotion Authority," Government Accountability Office, GAO-08-59, November 2007.

Gates, Robert, and Jose Manuel Santos. "Colombia's Gains are America's Too," *New York Times,* July 23, 2008.

Gibson, Martha. *Conflict Amid Consensus in American Trade Policy,* (Washington, D.C.: Georgetown University Press, 2000).

Goldfinger, Nathaniel. "What Labor Wants on Trade," *New York Times,* March 4, 1973.

Goodin, Robert E. "Enfranchising all affected interests, and its alternatives," *Philosophy & Public Affairs,* 35:1, 2007.

Grimmett, Jeane J. "Why Certain Trade Agreements are Approved as Congressional-Executive Agreements Rather than as Treaties," Congressional Research Service Report 97-896, Feb. 8, 2005. Available at: http://fpc.state.gov/documents/organization/9553.pdf. Accessed on July 22, 2008.

Gugliotta, Guy. "Fast Track Gives Marathoners Slip; Speaker Pulled Trade Bill After Long Night of House Bluff, Counterbluff," *Washington Post,* Nov. 11, 1997.

Halloran, Richard. "GATT Talks Begin to Liberalize World Trade," *New York Times,* Sept. 13, 1973.

Hennig, Jutta. "Rangel Signals Possible Limited Fast-Track for Doha Round," *Inside U.S. Trade,* Feb. 2, 2007.

Holt, W. Stull. *Treaties Defeated by the Senate,* (Baltimore: Johns Hopkins Press, 1933).

Homan, Timothy. "House GOP Frames Colombia Free-Trade Deal as a National Security Issue," *CQ Today,* April 3, 2008. Available at: http://www.reuters.com/article/pressRelease/idUS192570+03-Apr-2008+PRN20080403. Accessed on July 22, 2008.

HTWG. Letter from the House Trade Working Group to U.S. Trade Representative Ron Kirk, Jan. 10, 2010. Available at http://michaud.house.gov/press-release/house-trade-working-group-requests-meeting-ustr-trans-pacific-partnership-fta.

IFG. International Forum on Globalization. *Alternatives to Economic Globalization,* (San Francisco: Berrett Koehler, 2004).

IFTC. Iowa Fair Trade Campaign questionnaires to candidates, released Dec. 28, 2007, at http://www.iowafairtrade.org/candidates.php, accessed June 6, 2008.

IN. "Without His Signature," *Independent,* Aug. 30, 1894.

Irwin, Douglas A. "The Nixon Shock after Forty Years: The Import Surcharge Revisited," NBER Working Paper No. 17749, January 2012.

Issa, Darrell. "Congressman Issa Releases Statement About Denial of Admission to Upcoming Trans-Pacific Partnership Negotiations," July 1, 2012. Available at: http://issa.house.gov/press-releases/2012/07/congressman-issa-releases-statement-about-denial-of-admission-to-upcoming-trans-pacific-partnership-negotiations/. Accessed Feb. 26, 2013.

IUT. "Kantor Pledges Presidential Focus on NAFTA Passage Once Side Pacts Done," *Inside U.S. Trade,* March 19, 1993.

IUT. "House Republicans drop fast-track renewal from budget bill," *Inside U.S. Trade,* Oct. 20, 1995a.

IUT. "Richardson Makes New Effort to Break House Fast-Track Deadlock," *Inside U.S. Trade,* Dec. 1, 1995b.

IUT. "Fast-Track to be a Key Priority for Bush, Spokesman Says," *Inside U.S. Trade,* Jan. 12, 2001a.

IUT. "House Democrats attack Republican push on clean fast-track bill", *Inside U.S. Trade,* June 15, 2001b.

IUT. "Nine Key Democrats Warn Against Partisan Fast-Track Strategy," *Inside U.S. Trade,* June 22, 2001c.

IUT. "Levin Delays Introduction of Fast-Track Trade Principles," *Inside U.S. Trade,* Aug. 3, 2001d.

IUT. "Outline of House Democrat Fast-Track Bill," *Inside U.S. Trade,* Oct. 5, 2001e.

IUT. "House fast-track compromise efforts faltering, new talks uncertain," *Inside U.S. Trade,* Nov. 9, 2001f.

IUT. "House Textile Fast-Track Votes Won by Limiting CBI Fabric Benefits," *Inside U.S. Trade,* Dec. 7, 2001g.

IUT. "Business looks to curtail Baucus provisions on investor-state," *Inside U.S. Trade,* Dec. 14, 2001h.

IUT. "Daschle Signals Willingness to Kill Dayton-Craig After Bush Warning," *Inside U.S. Trade,* May 17, 2002a.

IUT. "Kerry Defeat Boosts Industry Case in Interagency Debate," *Inside U.S. Trade,* May 24, 2002b.

IUT. "Final fast-track deal weakens Dayton-Craig trade remedy provisions," *Inside U.S. Trade,* Aug. 2, 2002c.

IUT. "USTR cool to Finance labor amendment to Oman draft FTA bill," *Inside U.S. Trade,* May 19, 2006a.

IUT. "Implementing Legislation Can Only Be Submitted Once Under Fast Track," *Inside U.S. Trade,* Nov. 10, 2006b.

IUT. "Business Warns Administration Against Forcing Vote on Colombia FTA," *Inside U.S. Trade,* Feb. 8, 2008.

IUT. "U.S. Delays TPP Talks to Allow Obama Cabinet Members to Take Office," Feb. 24, 2009a.

IUT. "House Democrats Press Pelosi To Refrain From Panama FTA Vote," *Inside U.S. Trade,* May 22, 2009b.

IUT. "Kirk Says Administration Will Seek Fast Track Authority, Predicts Approval," *Inside U.S. Trade,* Dec. 19, 2009c.

IUT. "Kirk: USTR Wants to Continue TPP Negotiations, Panama Work Ongoing," *Inside U.S. Trade,* May 18, 2009d.

IUT. "Administration Gave Congress Little Notice Of Korea FTA Announcement," *Inside U.S. Trade,* July 2, 2010a.

IUT. "USTR Sees Korea FTA, 2010 Changes As Separate Legal Agreements," *Inside U.S. Trade,* May 15, 2011a.

IUT, "House, Senate Set To Hold Votes On FTAs On Oct. 12 Before Lee Visit," *Inside U.S. Trade,* Oct. 7, 2011b.

IUT. "Kirk Says Congressional TPP Consult Will Include Fast-Track Discussion," *Inside U.S. Trade,* Dec. 2, 2011c.

IUT. "131 House Dems Criticize Direction Of TPP; Demand Greater Transparency," *Inside U.S. Trade,* June 28, 2012a.

IUT. "Wyden, Issa Join Forces In Latest Effort For More Transparency In TPP," *Inside U.S. Trade,* Sep. 6, 2012b.

Jackson, John. "The General Agreement on Tariffs and Trade in U.S. Domestic Law," *Michigan Law Review,* 66, 1967.

Jackson, John, and Jean-Victor Louis and Mitsuo Matsushita. "Implementing the Tokyo Round: Legal Aspects of Changing International Economic Rules," *Michigan Law Review,* 81, 1982.

Jackson, John. "World Trade Rules and Environmental Policies: Congruence or Conflict?" *Washington & Lee Law Review,* 49, Fall 1992.

Jackson, John. "The Great 1994 Sovereignty Debate: United States Acceptance and Implementation of the Uruguay Round Results," *Columbia Journal of Transnational Law,* 36, 1997.

Jeffers, Gromer, and Christopher Lee. "Sparks Fly with Kirk, Bentsen," *Dallas Morning News,* March 8, 2002.

Johnston, Louis D., and Samuel H. Williamson, "What Was the U.S. GDP Then?" *Measuring Worth,* 2008.

Jones, Brendan. "U.S. Trade Policy Faces an Airing in Congress," *New York Times*, July 5, 1973.

Jonquieres, Guy de. "Network Guerillas," *Financial Times*, April 30, 1998.

Judis, John B. *The Paradox of American Democracy*, (New York: Taylor & Francis, 2001).

Kaufman, Robert. *Henry M. Jackson: A Life in Politics*, (Seattle, University of Washington Press, 2000).

Kazin, Michael. *The Populist Persuasion*, (Ithaca: Cornell University Press, 1995).

Kirk, Ronald. "Next Steps on the Trade Agenda", Remarks by Ambassador Ron Kirk, U.S. Trade, Delivered at United States Chamber of Commerce, May 18, 2009. (Transcript on file at Public Citizen.)

Kirk, Ron. Letter from U.S. Trade Representative Ron Kirk to House of Representatives Speaker Nancy Pelosi, U.S. Trade Representative, Dec. 14, 2009. Available at: http://www.ustr.gov/webfm_send/1559.

Koh, Harold Hongju. "Congressional controls on presidential trade policymaking after INS v. Chadha," *NYU Journal of International Law & Politics*, 18, 1986.

Koh, Harold Hongju. "The Fast Track and United States Trade Policy," *Brooklyn Journal of International Law*, 18:1, 1992.

Labaree, Benjamin Woods. *The Boston Tea Party* (Boston: Northeastern University Press, 1979).

LAT. "Quota Rider Fails in Vote on Trade Bill," *Los Angeles Times*, July 17, 1973.

Laxer, Gordon, and John Dillon. "Over a Barrel: Exiting From NAFTA's Proportionality Clause," Canadian Center for Policy Alternatives Report, May 2008.

Lewis, Charles. "The NAFTA-Math: Clinton Got His Trade Deal, but How Many Millions Did It Cost the Nation?" *Washington Post*, Dec. 26, 1993.

Linarelli, John. "International Trade Relations and the Separation of Powers Under the United States Constitution," *Duke Journal of International & Comparative Law*, 13, Winter 1995.

Lofgren, Zoe. Letter from Rep. Zoe Lofgren to U.S. Trade Representative Ron Kirk, Sep. 20, 2012. Available at: http://lofgren.house.gov/images/stories/pdf/letter%20to%20ustr%20from%20rep.%20lofgren%20re%20tpp%20092012.pdf.

Lugar, Sen. Richard (R-Ind.). Congressional Press Release, April 7, 2008. Available at http://lugar.senate.gov/press/record.cfm?id=295658. Accessed on July 15, 2008.

MacArthur, John R. *The Selling of "Free Trade,"* (New York: Hill & Wang, 2000).

Marks, Matthew J., and Harald B. Malmgren, "Negotiating nontariff distortions to trade," *Law & Policy in International Business*, 7:2, 1975.

Mastel, Greg, and Hal Shapiro. "Fast Track Forever?" *The International Economy*, Summer 2006.

Matusow, Allen J. *Nixon's Economy: Booms, Busts, Dollars & Votes*, (Lawrence: University Press of Kansas, 1998).

McGrane, Victoria. "Rangel Puts Doha-Specific, Restricted Fast Track for Bush on the Table," *CQ Today*, April 17, 2007.

McKinsey, Philip. "Nixon to Get Trade Power – At a Price," *Christian Science Monitor*, April 18, 1973.

MH. "White House Ordered to Hire Environmentalist," *Miami Herald,* Jan. 22, 2003.

National Journal. United Technologies / *National Journal* Poll, Oct. 13-16, 2011. Available at: http://www.nationaljournal.com/daily/in-both-parties-a-schism-on-trade-20111017 .

NCSL. "Policies for the Jurisdiction of the Labor and Economic Development Committee: Free Trade and Federalism," National Conference of State Legislatures, adopted August 2012. Available at http://www.ncsl.org/state-federal-committees.aspx?tabs=854,15,695.

Nelson, Chris. "Fast Track Wins… in 'Overtime,'" *Nelson Report,* Dec. 6, 2001.

NFTC. "NFTC Releases Draft Trade Negotiating Authority Act of 2009," National Foreign Trade Council Press Release, July 10, 2008. Available at: http://www.nftc.org/newsflash/newsflash.asp?Mode=View&articleid=1969&Category=All . Accessed July 25, 2008.

Nichols, John. "Colombia Trade Fight is a Human Rights Test," *The Nation,* April 11, 2008.

NYT. "Reciprocity Treaties with Other Countries," *New York Times,* Nov. 24, 1901.

NYT. "Bailey Begins Attack on the Cuban Bill," *New York Times,* Dec. 15, 1903.

NYT. "Walsh Opens Fight on Flexible Tariff," *New York Times,* May 9, 1922a.

NYT. "Would Bar Congress from Tariff Cutting," *New York Times,* Sept. 18, 1922b.

Obama, Barack. Letter from presidential candidate Barack Obama to the Iowa Fair Trade Campaign, Dec. 26, 2007. Available at: http://www.citizen.org/documents/Obama_IFTC.pdf.

O'Connor, Patrick, and Victoria McGrane, "Bush Sends Colombia Deal on Fast Track," *Politico,* April 7, 2008.

O'Halloran, Sharyn. *Politics, Process and American Trade Policy,* (University of Michigan Press, 1994.)

Palmer, Doug. "Lawmakers, citing Obama, urge U.S. redo trade deals," *Reuters,* June 4, 2008.

Public Citizen. "Prosperity Undermined During Era of Fast Tracked NAFTA and WTO Model Trade Agreements," updated 2013. Available at http://www.citizen.org/documents/ProsperityUnderminedFINAL.pdf.

Public Citizen. "Trade Advisory Committees: Privileged Access for Polluters," Public Citizen Report, December 1991. At http://www.citizen.org/documents/TradeAdvisoryCmtesReport_Hilliard1991.pdf. Accessed July 18, 2008.

Public Citizen. "Table of Foreign Investor-State Cases and Claims under NAFTA and Other U.S. Trade Deals," Public Citizen, January 2013. Available at: http://www.citizen.org/documents/investor-state-chart.pdf.

Pelosi. "Pelosi, Hoyer, Rangel, and Levin Statement on Trade," Congressional Press Release, June 29, 2007.

Perlstein, Rick. *Nixonland,* (New York: Scribner, 2008).

Pier, Carol. "Workers' rights provisions in fast track authority, 1974-2007: an historical perspective and current analysis," *Indiana Journal of Global Legal Studies,* 13:1, Winter 2006.

Politi, James. "House derails Colombia trade agreement," *Financial Times,* April 10, 2008.

Raghavan, Chakravarthi. *Recolonization: GATT, the Uruguay Round & the Third World,* (London: Zed Books, 1990a).

Raghavan, Chakravarthi. "Establishment of MTO on Agenda of Brussels Meeting," *Third World Network's SUNS- South North Development Monitor*, Nov. 27, 1990b.

Remini, Robert V. *The House,* (Washington, D.C.: Smithsonian Books, 2006).

RMSN. "Ralph Nader's 12-question 'GATT Challenge' Helped State's Republican Senator Decide to Oppose Treaty," *Rocky Mountain State News*, Dec. 4, 1994.

Runningen, Roger. "Obama Signs Trade Deals With Three Nations," *Bloomberg,* Oct. 21, 2011.

Salas, Carlos. "Between Unemployment and Insecurity in Mexico: NAFTA Enters Its Second Decade," Economic Policy Institute Report, 2006.

Sandbrook, Dominic. *Eugene McCarthy and The Rise and Fall of American Liberalism* (New York: Anchor Books, 2005).

Schaller, Thomas. *Whistling Past Dixie,* (New York: Simon & Schuster, 2006.)

Schlesinger, Jr., Arthur M. *The Coming of the New Deal,* (New York: Mariner, 1958).

Schondelmeyer, Stephen W. "The Extension of GATT Patent Extension on Currently Marketed Drugs," PRIME Institute, University of Minnesota, March 1995.

Schmickle, Sharon. "In a fast - track gamble, Clinton pushes for vote in House today," *Minneapolis Star Tribune,* Nov. 7, 1997.

Schwab, Susan. "Letter from Susan C. Schwab to the Honorable Nancy Pelosi, Speaker, U.S. House of Representatives," Sep. 22, 2008a. Available at: http://ustraderep.gov/assets/World_Regions/Southeast_Asia_Pacific/Trans-Pacific_Partnership_Agreement/Other_Documents_(Letters,_etc)/asset_upload_file775_15142.pdf

Schwab, Susan. "Letter from Susan C. Schwab to the Honorable Nancy Pelosi, Speaker, U.S. House of Representatives", December 30, 2008b, Available at: http://ustraderep.gov/assets/World_Regions/Southeast_Asia_Pacific/Trans-Pacific_Partnership_Agreement/Other_Documents_(Letters,_etc)/asset_upload_file152_15321.pdf

Sek, Lenore. "Trade Promotion Authority (Fast-Track Authority for Trade Agreements): Background and Developments in the 107th Congress," Congressional Research Service Issue Brief 10084, Nov. 16, 2001. Available at: http://www.opencrs.cdt.org/document/RL31844. Accessed July 22, 2008.

Serin, William. "For Roche of G.M. happiness is a 10% surcharge," *New York Times,* Sept. 12, 1971.

SF. Senate Finance Committee Hearings on H.R. 1612, March 16-April 6, 1951.

SF. Senate Finance Committee Hearings on H.R. 11970, July 24, 1962.

SF. Senate Finance Committee Hearings on H.R. 10710, March 4 – April 10, 1974.

Shabecoff, Philip. "Feeding meat to the lions," *New York Times,* Sept. 12, 1971.

Shabecoff, Philip. "President Plans to Seek 'Options' in Trade Talks," *New York Times,* Feb. 20, 1973.

Shapiro, Hal, and Lael Brainard, "Trade promotion authority formerly known as Fast Track," *George Washington International Law Review,* 35, 2003.

Shapiro, Hal. *Fast Track: A Legal, Historical, and Political Analysis,* (Ardsley, N.Y.: Transnational Publishers, 2006).

Shoch, James. "Contesting globalization: organized labor, NAFTA and the 1997 and 1998 fast-track fights," *Politics & Society,* 28:1, March 2000.

148

Shoch, James. *Trading Blows: Party Competition and U.S. Trade Policy in a Globalizing Era,* (Chapel Hill: University of North Carolina Press, 2001.)

Silk, Leonard. "Checkmated Democrats," *New York Times,* Sept. 8, 1971.

Sim, Edmund W. "Derailing the fast track for international trade agreements," *Florida International Law Journal,* 5, 1990.

Skidmore, Dave. "Sen. Brown Takes Nader's GATT Quiz, Earns Perfect Score," *Associated Press,* Nov. 28, 1994.

Slevin, Chris, and Todd Tucker. "The Fair Trade Sweep," *The Democratic Strategist,* January 2007. Available at: http://www.citizen.org/documents/SlevinTucker-TheFairTradeSweep.pdf. Accessed July 22, 2008.

Smith, Carolyn C. "Trade Promotion Authority and Fast-Track Negotiating Authority for Trade Agreements: Major Votes," Congressional Research Service Report RS21004, Jan. 31, 2007.

Solberg, Carl. *Hubert Humphrey: A Biography,* (New York: W.W. Norton, 1985).

Stokes, Bruce. "A Victory Yes, But For How Long?" *National Journal,* Aug. 2, 2002.

Strawbridge, Jamie. "Peru FTA Vote Shows Strong Democratic Support, But No Majority," *Inside U.S. Trade,* Nov. 9, 2007.

Swanson, Ian. "Baucus Shifts Course on Fast Track," *The Hill,* April 13, 2007.

Sweeney, John. "Colombia: No Rights, No Trade," *Washington Post,* April 14, 2008.

Tefft, Sheila. "Trade strength seen in services," *Chicago Tribune,* Nov. 26, 1980.

Teixeira, Ruy, and Joel Rogers. *America's Forgotten Majority,* (New York: Basic Books, 2000).

TIME. "Starting the Drive," *Time Magazine,* Dec. 15, 1961.

Tribe, Laurence H. "Taking Text and Structure Seriously: Reflections on Free-Form Method in Constitutional Interpretation," *Harvard Law Review,* 108, April 1995.

Tucker, Todd, and Brandon Wu and Alyssa Prorok. "Trade Wars: Revenge of the Myth," Public Citizen Report, June 2005. Available at: http://www.citizen.org/publications/release.cfm?ID=7391&secID=2057&catID=126. Accessed July 22, 2008.

Tucker, Todd. "Dangerous CAFTA Liaisons," Public Citizen Report, February 2006a. Available at: http://www.citizen.org/documents/CAFTA_Liaisons_Report.pdf. Accessed July 30, 2008.

Tucker, Todd. "Election 2006: No to staying the course on trade," Public Citizen Report, November 2006b. Available at: http://www.citizen.org/hot_issues/issue.cfm?ID=1471. Accessed July 22, 2008.

Tucker, Todd, and Mary Bottari and Lindsey Pullen. "Santa's Sweatshop: Made in D.C. With Bad Trade Policy," Public Citizen Report, December 2007. Available at: http://www.citizen.org/publications/release.cfm?ID=7554. Accessed July 22, 2008.

Tucker, Todd, and Mary Bottari. "Presidential Candidates' Key Proposals on Health Care and Climate Will Require WTO Modifications," Public Citizen Report, February 2008. Available at: http://www.citizen.org/publications/release.cfm?ID=7569. Accessed July 22, 2008.

Tucker, Todd. "Election 2008: Fair Trade Gets an Upgrade," Public Citizen Report, November 2008. Available at: http://www.citizen.org/trade/politics/. Accessed Jan. 8, 2009.

Tucker, Todd. "Election 2010: The Best Defense Was a Fair Trade Offense," Public Citizen

Report, November 2010. Available at: http://www.citizen.org/documents/2010_Election_Trade_Report.pdf. Accessed Jan. 6, 2012.

Tucker, Todd. "A Bad Trade," *Foreign Policy,* April 18, 2011. Available at: http://www.foreignpolicy.com/articles/2011/04/18/a_bad_trade. Accessed Jan. 19, 2012.

Tucker, Todd and Lori Wallach. "Obama's Wheel and Deal," *American Prospect,* Oct. 31, 2011. Available at: http://prospect.org/article/obamas-wheel-and-deal. Accessed Jan. 19, 2012.

UNCTAD. "UNCTAD and WTO: A Common Goal in a Global Economy," United Nations Conference on Trade and Development, TAD/INF/PR/9628, Aug. 10, 1996. Available at: http://www.unctad.org/Templates/webflyer.asp?docid=3607&intItemID=2298&lang=1. Accessed July 22, 2008.

USITC. *Reciprocity and Commercial Treaties,* (Washington, D.C.: U.S. Tariff Commission, 1919).

USTR, "Increasing U.S. Exports, Creating American Jobs: Engagement with the Trans-Pacific Partnership," USTR Factsheet, Nov. 13, 2009a. Available at: http://www.ustr.gov/about-us/press-office/blog/2009/november/increasing-us-exports-creating-american-jobs-engagement-tra. Accessed Feb. 26, 2013.

USTR. Request for Comments and Notice of Public Hearing: Proposed Trans-Pacific Partnership Free Trade Agreement," Federal Register, (Volume 74, Number 15), Jan. 26, 2009b. Available at: http://www.thefederalregister.com/d.p/2009-01-26-E9-1515.

USTR. "The President's Trade Policy Agenda," USTR Document, Feb. 27, 2009c. Available at: http://www.ustr.gov/sites/default/files/uploads/reports/2009/asset_upload_file810_15401.pdf. Accessed Jan. 19, 2012.

Vaughan, Martin. "US-Peru Trade Deal The First Test Of Renegotiated IP Provisions" *Intellectual Property Watch, Nov. 5, 2007.* Available at: http://www.ip-watch.org/weblog/index.php?p=811. Accessed July 22, 2008.

Wallach, Lori, and Patrick Woodall. *Whose Trade Organization?* (New York: New Press, 2004).

Wallach, Lori, and Todd Tucker. "The Myth of Mode 4 and the U.S. H1-B Program," Public Citizen Memo, March 2006. Available at: http://www.citizen.org/documents/Mode_Four_H1B_Visa_Memo.pdf. Accessed July 24, 2008.

Waxman, Henry. "Remarks on the 5th Anniversary of the May 10 Agreement," May 10, 2012. Available at: http://democrats.energycommerce.house.gov/sites/default/files/documents/Statement-Waxman-May-10-Agreement-2012-5-10.pdf.

Weisbrot, Mark, and Dean Baker and David Rosnick. "The Scorecard on Development: 25 Years of Diminished Progress," *International Journal of Health Services,* 36:2, 2006.

Wertkin, Jeffrey. "Reintroducing Compromise to the Nondelegation Doctrine," *Georgetown Law Journal,* April 2002.

Wilentz, Sean. *The Age of Reagan: A History, 1974-2008,* (New York: Harper, 2008).

Wilson, Theresa. "Who Controls International Trade? Congressional Delegation of the Foreign Commerce Power," *Drake Law Review,* 47, 1998.

WM. Ways & Means Committee, Hearing on H.R. 8430, March 8-14, 1934.

WM. Ways & Means Committee, Hearing on H.R. 6960, April 27-29, 1965.

WM. Ways & Means Committee, Hearing on H.R. 6767, May 9-June 15, 1973a.

WM. Ways & Means Committee, "Report on Trade Reform Act of 1973," House Report No. 93-571, Oct. 10, 1973b.

WM. Ways & Means Committee, Hearing on Legislation Necessary to Implement the Multilateral Trade Agreement Concluded in Geneva, April 23-27, 1979.

WP. "Passed by a Big Vote," *Washington Post,* Dec. 17, 1903.

WP. "Mr. Nixon's Trade Bill," *Washington Post,* April 13, 1973.

WTO. *World Trade Report 2007,* (Geneva: World Trade Organization, 2008).

Yoo, John C. "Laws as Treaties? The Constitutionality of Congressional-Executive Agreements," *Michigan Law Review,* 99:4, February 2001.

Zelizer, Julian. *Taxing America: Wilbur D. Mills, Congress and the State, 1945-1975,* (Cambridge: Cambridge University Press, 1998).

Zelizer, Julian. *On Capitol Hill,* (Cambridge: Cambridge University Press, 2000).